D1564364

Our Tomorrows Never Came

OUR TOMORROWS NEVER CAME

Etunia Bauer Katz

Fordham University Press
New York • 2000

Library of Congress Cataloging-in-Publication Data
Katz, Etunia Bauer, 1922–
    Our tomorrows never came / Etunia Bauer Katz.
       p.   cm.
    ISBN 0-8232-2031-1 (hardcover)—ISBN 0-8232-2032-X (pbk.)
       1. Katz, Etunia Bauer, 1922–   2. Jews—Ukraine—Buchach—
Biography.   3. Holocaust, Jewish (1939–1945)—Ukraine—
Buchach—Personal narratives.   4. Buchach (Ukraine)—
Biography.   I. Title.

DS135.U43 K384 2000
940.53'18'092—dc21   00-028762

Printed in the United States of America
00   01   02   03   04   5   4   3   2   1
First Edition

In memory of my parents, Anschel and Frieda Bauer, my sister, Bronia, and my brothers, Monio, Rumek, and Molus

CONTENTS

ELEGY

Now, at last, come her good-byes
to those she loved,
though they have lain,
these many years,
in that far field
far from her eyes.

She always sees
their eyes, their dreams,
as once they were,
when hearts and hopes
were life to her.

Now, at last, are horrors told,
for she still hears
their silent cries
and feels their touch
in memory.
Not one grew old.

Time had ended.
All she has are
faded faces,
vanished voices,
lost embraces.

Now, at last, these pages mark
those restless graves
where no one comes,
and no one prays,
and no one weeps,
in day or dark.

Remember them,
for they were loved;
their joys were brief.
They are not lost
if only we
remember them.

—Frieda Libbe

FOREWORD

This haunting and illuminating Holocaust memoir by Etunia Bauer Katz is a welcome addition to the ever-growing number of survivor autobiographies published in recent years. Written as a loving memorial to the author's parents, sister, and brothers, the book painstakingly recounts the Bauer family's desperate plight as they fled and hid from the Nazis and their accomplices. Writing it also proved cathartic to the author, for whom the project opened a "chest of memories . . . locked for nearly half a century" and helped calm "the aching memories of horror and catastrophe."

The tale as it unfolds is an unremitting tragedy. Members of the Bauer family lived through one harrowing experience after another as they tried to evade Nazi shootings, roundups, pogroms, forced labor conscription, ghettoization, and deportations. Although they narrowly escaped death on innumerable occasions, ultimately all perished save Etunia.

What gives this book its particular poignancy and force—apart from the intrinsically wrenching events themselves—is the gifted author's prose, which is suffused with memorable metaphors, passion, and acute human understanding. Moreover, like the anguished medieval European Jewish chronicles lamenting the group traumas of their time, this memoir meshes the author's objective narrative voice with her experiences as narrative subject, all the while interpolating her ruminations about life and especially her theological and moral wrestling with God. Although this contemporary work shows greater fidelity to historical accuracy than do the medieval chronicles, it nonetheless shares with them their engaged, introspective style of historical reporting.

Like most Holocaust experiences, Katz's, too, were marked by sudden, fateful transitions from a remembered idyllic past, when life was essentially tranquil, to a threatening present replete with brutality and terror. As the book opens, we are introduced to the

Bauers, a pious Polish Jewish family that was close knit, educated and, by the standards of the day, quite well-off. Etunia and her twin brother, Monio, were born in 1922 to Anschel and Frieda Bauer. The twins had an older sister, Bronia, and a younger set of twin brothers, Rumek and Molus. In the early 1930s, the family relocated to the East Galician town of Buczacz in the province of Tarnopol, once home of the Nobel Laureate S. Y. Agnon, among other Jewish notables. Anschel Bauer had leased and farmed a country estate of eight hundred acres which, Katz recalls, offered the children a life of "pastoral contentment and peace," filled with gamboling in the orchards, berry picking, and other joyful pleasures. This boundless happiness was initially shattered by the mysterious, premature death of her mother, Frieda, in 1938, at age forty-six, an ominous presentiment of the drastic new circumstances soon to engulf the family and all the Jews in the region.

The changes came swiftly and abruptly. In the wake of the onset of World War II, East Poland was seized by the Soviets in accordance with the secret deal between Hitler and Stalin to split Poland between them. The Bauers fled their farm, fearful of being transported to Siberia. With the subsequent German invasion of the Soviet Union in June 1941, East Poland fell to the Nazis, and the physical deprivation and political instability under the Soviets deteriorated into an unmitigated living hell. The description of this hell and how it impinged on the Bauer family and on Katz herself constitutes the core of this memoir.

The Nazis entered Buczacz on July 5, 1941, and the period of ruthless destruction began. Katz's twin brother, Monio, was among the four hundred to five hundred Jewish men shot in the first Nazi massacre on August 26, 1941. Subsequently, her younger twin brothers were caught in a raid and slated to be transported to the Borki labor camp. In this case, the Nazis were open to bribery and held the twins, along with many others, for ransom. Using money and personal connections with Gentile acquaintances, Anschel Bauer eventually succeeded in freeing his children.

Money, other valuables, and a network of Gentile connections became critical resources to the Bauers as they hid from Nazi authorities in barns, chicken coops, open grain fields, abandoned huts, and even in their own former manor house, which was sometimes occupied. With lyric intensity, Katz conveys the utter despair and palpable terror felt by her and her loved ones as they wandered from place to place, never quite certain whether a decision made to secure safety would in fact prove true or become a trap. One aspect of their wanderings, however, was consistent: for safety, food, and lodging, they most often depended on the assistance of Polish and Ukrainian friends, business associates, and workers Anschel Bauer had once hired on the farm. Some came to their aid out of pure friendship and without any desire for compensation; others required significant compensation. Still others turned their backs on the family altogether. The spectrum from altruism to human insensitivity in all its complex manifestations is here for all to see and ponder.

In her Epilogue, the author describes aspects of her life after liberation and recounts the happy experience of meeting another Jewish survivor, Julian Katz, whom she eventually married. The narrative even shares some of his heroic tales of survival. The ending of this book, therefore, is uplifting: Katz was able to physically and spiritually reconstruct her life in America, blessed with children to carry on the family line and heritage. But one's joy is muted. The Bauers, like so many millions of Jews, were victims of the evil wishes and political power of human killers who succeeded only too well in devastating a people and its culture. And while this remarkable story calls upon us to remember the horrific past while taking heart from an extraordinary tale of human endurance and revival, it also calls upon us to mourn those who, like Job's children, were irretrievably lost.

BENNY KRAUT
Professor of History/Director of the
  Center for Jewish Studies
Queens College

MY CHILDREN'S REFLECTIONS

Zachor Shoah: Remember the Holocaust. A simple phrase, one well understood in the home of my youth. At the same time, it is a most difficult phrase to understand, for how does one remember that which was never discussed?

I lived in my parents' home for over seventeen years before I left for college, and in those seventeen years, not once did I hear my parents discuss their experiences, their struggles, their fight to survive the Holocaust. And yet, my sisters and I grew up with an understanding—a moral imperative: *Zachor Shoah!* Remember the Holocaust.

On the surface, ours was a normal American Jewish household: the neat house in the suburbs, my father, the proud businessman running his business in downtown New York City, my mother, the homemaker caring for her children and husband and making sure that homework was done and meals were served—doing her all to provide a loving, nurturing environment. And yet, it was hardly the typical American household. When the holidays would come and our friends would visit grandparents and aunts and uncles, our family circle was remarkably small. And when we asked about grandparents or our family, we were told that they died in the War, that they were killed by Hitler—but the "how" and the "why" were never explained, and somehow we knew better than to ask.

Being children of survivors set us apart. As much as our parents loved and cherished us, and strove to shelter us, they also placed demands upon us. Average was not acceptable; we were held to higher standards. A "99" on a school examination was not greeted with applause but with, "What happened to the other point?" My parents, my father especially, strove to make us strong—and at the time we did not understand why. In retrospect, he must have wanted us to be prepared for the world that he and our mother had experienced.

Without ever discussing their experiences in Hitler's Holocaust, my parents were able to raise three children who are imbued with the spirit of *Zachor Shoah*. Even as small children, we were aware of our Jewish identities and were vocal in defending those identities. We may not have been traditional observant Jews; in fact, I recall having my own dialogues with God as to how God could let the six million die. But we were mindful of our identities and heritage, if ignorant of our own particular family history.

I do not profess to know the triggering event for my mother to finally face the demons of her past and commit this history to paper. I do know that it must have taken a great deal of courage to do so—to relive the events of Hitler's Holocaust. I do know that when I received a copy of this manuscript, it took me over a year to work up the courage to read it—because this is the history of *my* family. And having read this history, I stand back in awe. I cannot imagine myself, as a teenage boy, having the courage and fortitude to survive what my mother and father went through. And not just to survive, but to come through it all and then pick up the pieces and begin life anew, learning to live and love again.

Of course, no communication between a child and a parent is complete without a disagreement. Mom, the title of your book, your history of our family, *Our Tomorrows Never Came*, applies to your parents, your sister, and your brothers. Yes, there were no tomorrows for them. Your tomorrows, however, did come. You survived and went on to build a new life, to have a family— children, grandchild. Your family continues to live through you and through us. We remember them and the loving memory will live forever. As I told you at your granddaughter's bat mitzvah, when she joined the family of adult Jews, it meant that we had won: we had defeated Hitler.

A word of thanks. As a child, I never knew my family. From the bottom of my heart, Mom, I thank you for introducing me to the heroes of my family: Anschel, Frieda, Bronia, Monio, Rumek, and Molus Bauer. I am proud to be a descendant of a family such as theirs, and I make them a promise. Now that I have met them, I will never let their memory die.

Zachor Shoah.

ARTHUR KATZ
New Milford, New Jersey
April 1999

Zachor Shoah: REMEMBER THE HOLOCAUST

As the faces began to disappear
and the lives began to fade,
we began to wonder whom to trust
and by whom we would be betrayed.

We were rounded up
and the trains were packed tight.
Fearful of our fate,
would we see the next day's light?

Dying of starvation,
we watched the mound of bodies slowly grow.
Would we live through the day?
No one could know.

After years of brutality
and fighting for life,
we were free to find each other:
parent and child, husband and wife.

However, we still must remember
all of the people we lost.
The threat to our heritage and spirit,
to recognize evil and fight it no matter what the cost.

Zachor Shoah: Remember the Holocaust

DEBBIE KATZ
April 1999

PREFACE

During the years of moral darkness that engulfed the world early in the twentieth century, all Jews in Europe found themselves under the shadow of death. Death was always at their heels, hunting them out and, finally, overpowering them.

Hitler, employing his vile weapons of hate, oppressed us with venomous cruelty and forced us into humiliating, degrading wretchedness. Physically and psychologically flogged, we suffered from the first to the last days of the Hitler era and, indeed, long afterward. Death was not a remote, abstract image; rather, it was a reality that was constantly with us. We suffered the meanness of a constricted existence, the horrors of the camps, *akcjas,* and desperation during years of concealment under intolerable conditions in abysmal hiding places. Fear—life-eroding fear such as only violent and predictably fatal persecution can create—was our fate.

Although this book is the history of my family, it also tells of the fate of Jews outside the death camps—a fate shared by thousands of families who fought desperately to survive in a conquered land dominated by Nazis and their collaborators. About one million Jews in Eastern Europe shared our experience and did not survive to tell their story. Now the pitiful remainder who are still alive must let the world know what happened before their generation of living witnesses passes away.

My family—along with one million other Jews who were not sent to the German concentration camps or death camps, but who were murdered in bunkers, ghettos, attics, sewers, forests, fields, and roads, escaping from one hiding place to another—was persecuted by Hitler and died. My twin brother, Monio, and 450 other Jews—the first victims of Hitler's attack on Jews in our town—were shot and thrown into a pit, a mass grave, somewhere in a nearby forest. They were wiped off the face of the earth, their grave unmarked—lost to their loved ones and the world. As for

my father, my sister, and my younger brothers, their bones were
scattered in the fields, plowed over by farmers, desecrated by
grazing cattle and dogs—their burial places, too, unnamed. Their
only markers are the tombstones in my heart.

My chronicle of our bitter experience might elicit a cry of
"Enough already, enough!"—the very sentiment that those of us
who lived through the experience have often expressed ourselves.
You, dear reader, might want to stop reading to avoid being assailed by another succession of brutal events.

But that would be like punishing the messenger who brings the
unpleasant news. I escaped from the killing fields and present here
an eyewitness account of the hateful and systematic destruction of
my people. I must finish telling my story, late as it is and demand-
ing and difficult as it is to tell. It was far worse to have lived it,
yet my message must be heard.

From the day the Nazis first occupied our city, fear gripped its
Jews and never let go. Actually, our fear began earlier, when Hitler came to power. At that time, however, he was perceived as
only a distant menace. First there was bewilderment and disbelief,
then fear of the unknown and uncertain future. Gradually, our
bewilderment and disbelief became a progressively dark, grinding,
devastating, and deadly fear of having no future at all. Then, as
the intensity of our terror mounted, it brought the destruction of
body, soul and, not infrequently, mind. Although hope and our
innate faith in God remained with us, our lives became a nightmare, one long fight to live, an existence tormented by fear that
ended in the diabolically organized extermination of most of us:
the Nazi "Final Solution."

—E.B.K.

ACKNOWLEDGMENTS

This book came to be written at the insistence of my cousin, Alicia Appleman-Jurman. "You must, you must . . . ," she urged me. Thank you, Alicia, for your persistence. Deep in my heart I knew I must tell the world "what they did to us," and encourage future generations to remember our night of despair. It is a duty of all the survivors.

With loving gratitude I remember my dear late husband, Julie, whose advice was of significant value. He had a keen and just sense of assessing the human condition.

The help of my daughters, Felice and Ruth, is greatly appreciated. Felice helped with comments, typing a first draft, editing, and photographing the old family photos. Ruth typed and retyped the manuscript, "dotting the i's and crossing the t's," eventually producing a final copy. I am grateful to them both.

For helping me organize and edit the manuscript, I am deeply grateful to Gabriel Appleman, Alicia's husband. My friend Dr. Celia Heller provided advice and encouragement that is also deeply appreciated. To my *lands*ladies (fellow survivors)—Hilda Miller Weitz, Regina Gertner, and Bronia Hofman Kahane, who supplemented my memories with their own remembered details about certain situations, I am ever so grateful.

The help of Jacqueline Philpotts, marketing director, my first contact with Fordham University Press, is acknowledged with special pleasure. She was always kind and had good advice at the ready.

I wish to thank Fordham University Press director Saverio Procario and editor Anthony Chiffolo for their favorable assessment and work on my book.

INTRODUCTION

> . . . and, behold, a stormy wind came out of the north,
> a great cloud, with a fire flashing up. . . .
>
> Ezekiel 1:4

> Attend unto my cry;
>   for I am brought very low.
> Deliver me from my persecutors;
>   for they are too strong for me.
>
> Psalm 142:6

"IHR MÜST ALLE STERBEN WEIL IHR JUDEN SEID"

So began our annihilation. With brutal passion Hitler hunted
down hundreds of thousands of Jews and humiliated, degraded,
and murdered us. The graves of a million Jews are scattered across
Europe—most of the massacres having been committed in Poland, especially the eastern region, the Ukraine and Russia, all the
way to Babi-Yar.

Years ago my young granddaughter, Debora, attended Hebrew
school and had classes in Holocaust history. One day her father
picked her up from school and the usual conversation between
parent and child followed. "What did you learn today?" her
father asked. "Well, the lesson was about Hitler and concentration
camps," Debora replied. "The teacher asked who had parents and
grandparents who are survivors, and I raised my hand and said I
do. Then she asked me, 'What camp were they in?' I said that my
grandparents were not in a camp, that they were in hiding, and
the teacher said, 'Then they are not survivors.' " She struggled to
continue: "But, but . . . they are, Daddy. I know they are. How
could she say that?" The child was confused. My son, her father,
saw that his daughter felt betrayed, as if her grandparents were
being denied a deserved recognition. Indignant, my son made an

illegal U-turn and returned to the school, where he enlightened the teacher and the principal with a Holocaust history lesson.

Later chapters tell the history of my family and our life-and-death struggle to survive. This chapter tells how a few of the one million Jewish victims struggled to survive, how they fought for their lives, and how they died outside the camps. If the dead could speak, each would tell a similar tale.

My sister, Bronia, told me this story when she returned from one of her dangerous visits to the city of Buczacz to recover more of our belongings, which we sold or traded to pay for our shelter. Although she usually reported unhappy events, this time her account included an element of comfort and pride, which slightly eased our grief. A young girl had been imprisoned with hundreds of Jews who had been caught in the streets and who were to be taken to a nearby hill to be shot. As she awaited the end of her misery, this young girl poured out her heart in a poem that she wrote on the wall of the prison. Her poem portrayed the heartbreak of the Jewish population as well as the sadism of the German enemy and their helpers.

After the first and second akcjas, genocidal murder of Jews was carried out on the hills and in the forests of Buczacz. Because there were always communication leaks between the *Judenrat* and the Gestapo, word of pending pogroms and news of any other good or bad events got circulated. This is how the remnants of the Jewish community knew about the prison poem.

Almost everyone in Buczacz, including our family, knew of the girl, whose name was Etka Miller. Her family was dignified and highly respected. Her father, Meyer, was a *shochet* and a scholar of the sacred books. He and his wife, a pious, kindhearted woman, provided their two sons and three daughters with a beautiful home. The oldest son, Shiye, survived in Siberia (he is now deceased) and the youngest daughter, Hilda, survived in hiding and, for a time, passed as a Christian. Etka was the oldest daughter.

She was a bright, *gimnazjum*-educated, brave, and intelligent girl. As her people were marched to the hills for the "final solution," Etka pushed herself to the front and began a speech. The Gestapo, surprised and curious, let her speak, but addressed her first: "Ihr müst alle sterben weil ihr Juden seid" ("You all must die because you are Jews"). Etka faced her executioners and said what she felt. "How will the world judge you, you murderers? Who are you to judge us? For thousands of years people like you tried to eradicate us, but they could not and never will." Her words, "Humanity, wake up . . . ," were interrupted as the sound of shots began. Then, as she continued, "You will be defeated," one of the Gestapo shot her in the mouth—and God bless her soul. All but one of the remaining Jews died in the storm of machine-gun fire that followed.

Leizer Bader, a fourteen-year-old youngster, found himself at the edge of the pit with the doomed crowd of fellow Jews. As he stood in front of his father, who embraced him tightly, the signal was given, the machine guns rattled, and the storm of bullets flew. When his father was hit, he toppled over Leizer and they both fell into the pit. Later, in the stillness of the night that followed the "storm," young Leizer crawled out of the grave uninjured but naked as a newborn child. He ran into the woods, fought on for his life, and survived.

As for my immediate family, I am the sole survivor. Of my extended family on my mother's side, only one brother survived, and then for only a few years, although he had been cruelly beaten. The rest of the family—grandparents, aunts, uncles, cousins—all are gone, whether they died in camps or in hiding, I do not know. Of my father's family (he had eight siblings and they all had children), only my cousin Leah and my father's niece Giza remained; Giza survived with her family in Siberia. Some of my father's family died in Janowska Camp in Lwów, some in Belzec, some in akcjas; others died in ghettos or simply disappeared from the land of the living in the forests, fields, and hiding places in what was then Poland.

A few weeks after my arrival in America, I was contacted by a Jacob Klonymus, through the secretary of the Buczacz Society *Landsmanschaft*; he was searching for his nephew, his brother's son. I remember how Mr. Klonymus held a small notebook, a diary of his brother's daily experiences during Hitler's rule in Poland—the pages damp from his tears. Sadly, I could not help Mr. Klonymus, but I knew his brother Aryeh's in-laws, the Hertzmans, through our neighbor, Mrs. Bienerowa. Her daughter was married to the brother of Malvina Hertzman, Aryeh's wife. Aryeh and Malvina Klonymus were professors in a Pinsk gimnazjum and had gone to

Buczacz to vacation at the Hertzmans' home. Stranded there during the War, Aryeh, Malvina, and their infant son, having survived the akcjas, hid from the enemy in a field owned by their in-laws' exceptionally devoted housemaid. Faithful and good as she was, the housemaid could not always bring food to them in the field for fear of neighborhood Jew-hunters. Rain or shine, in the heat of the day and the cold of night, the family endured hunger and thirst. In the absence of milk, their infant son had to lick the moisture of morning dew from leaves.

All this was the second part of the family's misery, the first having been their tormented existence in the city, where they lived through akcjas, typhus, hunger, and the beating of Aryeh in Chortków Prison. Several times they had to buy their lives from peasant extortionists who threatened to report them. As their money ran out, their housemaid helped them make arrangements to leave their infant son with another peasant woman, and they left for the forest. They wrote to a friend, a fellow professor, and asked him to notify his brother, Jacob, in the United States and to inform him of the whereabouts of the child in the event they were killed. Eventually, the couple was caught and murdered, the fellow professor informed the surviving brother in New York, and the housemaid forwarded the diary. After the War, Mr. Klonymus contacted the A.J.D.C. (American Joint Distribution Committee) search department in New York and, along with its corresponding agency in Warsaw, they searched for his nephew. The result of their investigation proved to be doubly tragic.

It seems that at the end of the War, in the tumultuous time of the evacuation of Buczacz and the vicinity, the woman who had taken the child—for a price, of course—had changed her mind and had returned the baby to Franka, the Hertzmans' housemaid. Somewhere during her travels, Franka, in turn, gave the child to a Ukrainian church, where the child's name was changed from Adam to Taras and he was raised in the Greek Orthodox faith. When investigators of the A.J.D.C. committee contacted the church, Taras, by that time a teenager, responded adamantly: "I am a Ukrainian. I do not want anything to do with Jews"—and the case was closed.

Another example of how Jews died outside the camps: I read in one of the reports on the Holocaust that many synagogues

were burned in the first weeks of Nazi rule. In a small town near
Kielce, the Gestapo ordered all Jews to assemble in the synagogue.
There they spread a Torah scroll in the center of the floor and
ordered the Jews to walk around it in a circle and spit on it. All
but one complied—that one a thief, robber, and cheat. "I did
many wrong things in my life," he said, "but this is one thing I
will not do, ever." After he was put through excruciating torture
in front of the other Jews, the synagogue was set on fire with all
the Jews inside.

As persecution and annihilation progressed in Buczacz, con-
spiratorial talk began, mainly in young Zionist circles. As the
Judenfrei program progressed, some Jews joined a lightly armed
Jewish partisan group, while others trickled into the forest to
hide. A pack of young men, desperate to live, dug themselves
into the bowels of the earth where they tried to remain alive. As
one of the survivors related after the War, they stole, bought, or
coerced food from former Christian neighbors, farmers, and kind
strangers. They even dared to return to town to "visit" a grocery.
Many were betrayed, however; some were caught during their
searches for food, and still more were discovered by local Jew-
hunters, who either shot them on the spot or turned them over
to the Gestapo.

In the summer of 1943 my cousin Alicia, while working in a
farmer's field, found her friend Ozio Friedlander huddled in a
ravine along with four other youths, all runaways from the nightmarish existence in the city. In exchange for food or occasional
shelter, they guarded the small Polish colony from nightly assaults
by the Ukrainians. Ozio survived but the rest did not.

I also read about the Bielski brothers who led a partisan group
in the Naliboki Forest. These escapees from the ghettos in towns
and cities endured the hardships of life in hiding. In spite of those
hardships, heartbreaks, dangers, and defeats, they fought on. For
them, it ended well; the Bielski partisans saved twelve hundred
Jews.

Several years after my arrival in the United States, I found that
the small gatherings of survivor friends in the Bronx always ended
with narrations of our War experiences. I recall listening to a tale
of a group of Jews who were foraging for food. After finding food

and eating it quickly, they were murdered. Years later, when I moved to Queens County in New York, I met another survivor, Mr. Mazur, who was the owner of the local kosher butcher store. He told me the same story and added that the men, about twenty of them, had been partisans in the forests of Wilno. On one of their trips for food, they raided a farmer's pantry, but because they were starving, they simply could not wait to return to the safety of their hiding place to eat. Instead, they sat down in the snow in a field some distance from the farm ("sadly and stupidly," as the survivor said) to have a picnic. The farmer, along with a posse of friends, followed the men's footprints, found them at their feast, and shot them. The man who related this story to me had survived only because he had not been with that particular squad to procure food.

I am reminded of my friend Bronia Kahane (née Hofman), who was eight years old when the War broke out. Although she was of an age to attend regular school, Bronia was schooled in the arts of survival. With her father, mother, and brother, she lived through successive akcjas, hiding in attics, cellars, and bunkers. The first days of the German occupation did not bode well for Bronia and her family. Within a week of Hitler's rule, the Ukrainians were given a free hand and, from the beginning, many of them organized attacks on Jews. As a result, the Jews kept to their houses behind locked doors. One day, Bronia's mother answered a knock at the window to find their Ukrainian neighbor, a good friend for many years. They had shared meals in each other's home, had helped each other's family, and had let their children play together. This neighbor now called out, "Hancia, we are going to do this to you now," and made a slashing motion across her throat with her hand. Bronia's mother thought that the neighbor had come to warn her of danger.

They went into hiding and eventually found themselves in extreme situations, at the brink of death. When the family was betrayed, the Gestapo began raiding those houses where they were known to take refuge. In one of them, there was no choice but for Bronia and her mother to stand on a narrow ledge in a chimney while the stove was in use. Standing glued to the ledge, with their arms spread from wall to wall, they held on for dear life. The peasant wife kept feeding the fire as she cooked dinner, giving the impression that "there are no Jews here." The Gestapo and Ukrainians were relentless in their search because the villagers had informed them that Jews were in the vicinity.

Later, a Ukrainian betrayed Bronia and her mother. As an SS man led the mother and daughter away into the fields, he said to the Ukrainian gang, "I want to kill them myself." On the way to her death, however, Bronia's mother began speaking to the SS man in German and, because she had lived in Vienna, she was fluent in the language. As they spoke, it appeared that they had been neighbors on the same street in Vienna. As a result of their shared history, the SS man shot his weapon into the air and told the woman and her daughter to run. "Where are the bodies, the clothes, the blood?" asked the Ukrainians when the SS man returned to the gang, and because he could not produce evidence of death, the gang ran in pursuit. Fortunately, Bronia and her mother escaped and, after several days of hiding among corn stalks, they were found by a young Ukrainian who gave them a basket of food. Although the mob had spread the news of the event and it had become a sensation in the village, the young man saved the child and her mother. As a youngster, the Ukrainian had been a juvenile delinquent, a hoodlum. But because Bronia's grandfather had taken him into his care and had steered him toward better ways, he had grown into a decent adult—and he remembered that. Bronia's history continued with many miraculous escapes, but her father, mother, and brother eventually perished.

According to Yad VaShem, six million Jews died in the Holocaust; one million of them died outside the camps. The above mentioned Jews are only a small fraction of the million. Jews were murdered all over Poland, and other countries occupied by Hitler's forces, not only by advanced technology in the camps but also by uncivilized creatures, followers of evil.

Please, reader, light six candles in remembrance of the six million Jewish victims, *all of them!* Light the sixth candle for the Jews in hiding—for those who survived and the majority who perished. Let them, the million torn by canine and human dogs, be remembered.

BEFORE THE WAR

> Jerusalem remembereth
> in the days of her affliction
> and of her anguish,
> all the treasures that she had
> from the days of old. . . .
>
> Lamentations 1:7

The Bauer Family

Relation to author	Name	Year of birth	Polish name; nickname
Father	Osher Anschel	1881	
Mother	Fraidel Gaile	1892	
Sister	Rochel Brandl	1913	Bronia
Self	Ethel	1922	Emma; Etunia
Brother	Mordecai Dawid	1922	Markus; Monio
Brother	Abraham	1925	Roman; Rumek
Brother	Moshe Leib	1925	Mojzesz; Molus

Twins { (Ethel, Mordecai Dawid)

Twins { (Abraham, Moshe Leib)

Fascism in the Air

THERE WAS A RUMBLING in the air—a storm was brewing somewhere in the distance and the gathering clouds were floating in
our direction. We noted the clouds and felt the ominous breezes,
but a haze of doubt veiled our vision and we failed to note the
darkness. Gaining in intensity, growing ever sharper, the storm
eventually broke through the haze and burst forth, inundating
humanity in a sea of blood, pain, and death.

The time was the 1930s. Hitler was organizing his killing machinery, plotting and perfecting his schemes to conquer the world
and make it Aryan. Poland, instead of bracing herself and preparing a defense against Hitler, occupied itself with internal, more
urgent affairs, such as those concerning Jews. One of the most
pressing issues of the day was the *Shekhitah*, the Jewish ritual
slaughter of cattle required to make meat kosher for Jewish con-
sumption. The issue was debated in the legislature for years, periodically flaring up and spilling poison on the Jews. It was argued
that the Jewish way of slaughtering the animal by a single swift
cut of the cow's throat was not humane. The supporters of this
charge considered a bullet in the animal's head to be less cruel.
That method, of course, would render the meat unkosher. Day
by day the furor escalated and eventually reached a frenzied cres-
cendo. This, and similar internal disputes, allowed the bureau-
crats, as well as the general Polish population, to forget—or not
hear—the clatter as Hitler sharpened the knives with which he
would carve their land.

Anti-Semitism, always present in Poland, was now openly
manifested and, with Nazi propaganda feeding the flames of hate,
grew in force. For decades, the gimnazja and universities of Poland were filled with Jewish students; in fact, they formed a large
majority. In our town's gimnazjum some classes had, at one time,
been almost entirely Jewish, with only a sprinkling of Gentiles.

Suddenly a campaign began to draft farm and village youth into secondary schools, and Jewish enrollment was restricted. Throughout the 1930s, as anti-Semitism grew, fewer Jews were accepted into institutions of higher education. Then, in 1939, the last school year before the war, only one Jewish boy in our town was accepted into the gimnazjum. At the universities, Fascist thugs, the *Endecks,* beat the Jewish students, making it impossible for Jews to attend classes.

In the southeastern part of Poland, Podole, the Poles were in the minority. Although the area was officially part of Poland, the Ukrainian majority had always claimed the land to be theirs and part of the Ukraine—hence the centuries-old animosity between the two nationalities. Later, under German occupation, the Ukrainian majority was given civilian administrative power; thus, as Nazi collaborators, they had the advantage over the Poles. With time, Ukrainian irregular militias, the *Banderowcy,* increased in number and spread throughout the region. In the name of patriotism they terrorized the Poles and later fought—sabotaged—the Soviets. That patriotism, of course, called for "cleansing" the Jews from their land.

The Poles, a timid minority in this part of their land, were passive and generally indifferent to Jewish suffering; only a small number extended help to individual Jews, and many of those acted for financial gain. There were exceptions to this greed; a small minority gave unselfish help. If any Ukrainian helped, it was done with compensation as the most compelling, if not the only, motivation. But here, too, there were exceptions. In general, however, genuine sympathy and concern for Jews was hard to find.

Most of our support came from Polish and Polish-Ukrainian families; in fact, those villagers had vied for and felt privileged to have my father's friendship—before the War. In the sad years that were to come, they would support us with bread rations, however meager, which kept us alive—and we were thankful for that. To those sober individuals, those who went against the current and helped us, we are deeply grateful.

Buczacz, Our Hometown; Jósefówka, Our Home

BUCZACZ, our little city, was a beautiful, resort-like spot in a forested, mountainous area. At that time, Poland had sixteen province-states. Our city, larger than the surrounding towns, was the capital of the district (*powiat*) and, in turn, the district belonged to the province (*województwo*) of Tarnopol. The whole region— Tarnopol, Stanislawów, and Lwów provinces, comprising the most southeastern portion of Poland—was referred to as Eastern Galicia. It had been a part of Emperor Franz-Josef's Hapsburg Empire until 1918. In independent Poland after World War I, our region was called Podole, literally "under" the Karpaty Mountains. Buczacz was part of Poland until 1939; it was then ruled by the Soviets until 1941, and Germany's occupation lasted until 1944. After the War, the Ukraine remained a separate Soviet republic, and our region, always considered the Western Ukraine, was united with the eastern part. Today, as a result of the breakup of the USSR, Buczacz belongs to an independent Ukraine.

The population in the 1930s was about twenty-five thousand, half Jewish, half Polish and Ukrainian, with the latter being the majority. The River Strypa enveloped sections of the town in several S loops, rendering the community picturesque and peaceful. Buczacz is an old city, dating back to the fifteenth century. Confirming its age was the *ratusz*, the town hall, a stately Baroque structure that dominated all the other buildings located in the center of town. Other important buildings were the two public schools, the gimnazjum, the Sokół theater center (which contained the city library on the lower level), the courthouse, the movie house, churches, and cathedrals. There were also many small prayer and Torah study houses, or *shuls*. An architecturally exquisite structure that the Jewish community particularly cherished was the Great Synagogue, *die Groisseh Shul*.

The centuries-old Jewish community was a spiritually rich and vibrant society. Rabbi F. S. Willig led the rabbinical court, and the Jewish Community Council, or *Kehillah*, which was the authority representing the Jews, oversaw the affairs of Jewish life. The Council represented the Jews before the Polish authorities and managed the Jewish community by the law of the Talmud. (The Talmud, a body of interpretation and application of Torah law to everyday life, was developed over a span of centuries in the Jewish academies of Jerusalem and Babylon.)

The first president of the Kehillah was Dr. Emanuel Meringel; before the outbreak of the Second World War, he was succeeded by the much respected Mendel Reich. The Kehillah administered communal facilities, like the home for the aged, the orphanage, and the Jewish hospital. It also supervised religious schools, provided kosher meat, and, in general, served the Jewish community.

Although ours was a cohesive Jewish community, there was stratification among the well-to-do, the middle class, and the poor. Within those ranks, there were the Chasidic sect (Orthodox traditionalists of great piety and fervor, strictly observant of Torah teaching), the conservative ("Yiddish-home") Jews, and the secular. The intelligentsia had its own circle, where assimilated Jews predominated. For the most part, the Jews lived in the inner city, where they outnumbered the Christian citizenry. Jewish families also lived among the Christians in outlying neighborhoods and suburbs.

The city's central-area stores were primarily Jewish-owned, with a few exceptions such as the *Apteka,* a drugstore, and the ham-and-sausage dealers. When the stores were closed on the Jewish Sabbath, the town was "dead," which was deeply resented by the Gentiles and created a great deal of grumbling. Anti-Semitism surfaced, inadvertently or intentionally, in little incidents, the frequency and scale of which grew throughout the thirties. The local government officials were Polish citizens, and Jews approached these Polish office, school, and court officials cautiously, on "tiptoe," so to speak. Every Christmas Eve, the Jews would lock and bolt their doors and did not dare step outside, especially when carolers were going from house to house through the neighborhoods. It was not prudent to tempt fate—for to the Christians, Jews were generally considered Christ-killers, a fervently held belief encouraged by their priests. For a Jew to appear in person on this holy Christian night could be compared to a murderer defiantly appearing among the mourners of his victim.

The Christian population lived primarily in villas or cottages on the edge of town, although some resided in town in a *kamienica*, a three-to-four-story building usually owned by a Christian. The general population supported itself by various occupations: office executives, teachers, professors, clerks, police, court personnel, traders, merchants, craftspeople, and a few lawyers and doctors.

Sometimes anti-Semitic incidents occurred in Buczacz. For example, Chasidic Jews, dressed in their traditional black coats and fur hats, were often taunted by Christians, especially youngsters and young men. I also recall that when my mother asked Principal Keffermuller to exempt her children from school on the High Holy Days, the answer was a sharp "We don't observe Jewish holidays." Pain lingers, too, when I recall another incident of anti-Semitic behavior: My friend Regina Gertner, who was born in Buczacz and had married and moved to Tluste, arranged to bring her two-year-old daughter to a Polish woman at the height of the Nazi persecution. This woman was to take the child to the Chernovogrod cloister, which was near Tluste, and leave her on the steps. The nuns there soon discovered the child and took her in, believing her to be a foundling. Later, when Regina came to claim her daughter at the end of the War, she discovered that the child had been reared in a virulent anti-Semitic atmosphere, and the nuns did not want to relinquish her. The young girl spat at her mother and cursed her, using the usual ugly epithets, *Parszyna Zydówka* ("Mangy, dirty Jew"). Eventually, with the help of Soviet authorities, the child was returned to her mother and today the mother and daughter reside in the United States. The lost years, however, have left their scars.

The churches, too, were openly anti-Semitic. Yet when the Polish archbishop from Lwów came to Buczacz and the city government organized a great reception for him, a rabbi carried a Torah at the head of the Jewish delegation that was among the city's welcoming representatives. I was among the crowd of excited people—Christian and Jewish—that lined the streets for the parade and pomp of that event. I recall being quite impressed.

Most of the peasants and clergy of Buczacz perceived a Jew,

especially a merchant, to be a deceiver, a dishonest creature. The Gentile intelligentsia could be either dangerously anti-Semitic or honestly friendly.

Because of the predominance of the Ukrainian population in our area, the common language was Ukrainian (although Polish was the official language), so most Jews in Buczacz spoke fluent Ukrainian. Their Polish, however, was embarrassing and, as a result, the Poles treated the Jews' mangling of the language with deep disdain and anti-Semitic incivility. Only the assimilated Jews and those who associated socially with Poles spoke a perfect Polish.

In spite of these obstacles and the frustrating impediments of unwritten laws, Jewish life was vibrant. The Chasidim flocked to shuls for Torah study; the middle class (mainly merchants and craftsmen) thrived; the youth studied in public schools, Hebrew schools, Talmud-Torahs, schools for studying Torah, and the *cheders*. Less traditional "modern" youth attended the excellent Tarbut Hebrew school. There also were various circles, clubs, and organizations: Zionist, Socialist, small clandestine Communist cells, and academic and professional groups. All kept their members—adult and youth—active, but the fervor of the Zionist groups was especially vigorous.

This kind of Eastern European *shtetl* life has been described in S. Y. Agnon's books, and to read his work is to enjoy great literature. With humor, irony, wisdom, and deep insight into human life, Agnon's writing mourns the despair and poverty of his people. In his novel titled *A Guest for a Night,* for example, he describes the shtetl after World War I, when Buczacz was devastated by a Ukrainian nationalist, Petlura, Jews were murdered, and their homes were plundered. Agnon bewails the vanishing world of traditional values—the House of Study is empty. Given the key to the old shul, the empty House of Study, he remembers the old tradition of studying Torah, and he misses his friends who are gone. With the key, he hopes to reopen the House of Study, symbolizing for the new generation that they should continue their tradition of study and return to past values and faith. In *The Bridal Canopy* the reader travels with poor Reb Yudel and his God, and shares in the rabbi's warm and joyous feeling of bringing his daughter to the *chuppah* (bridal canopy). Agnon, a winner of the Nobel Prize for Literature, was born in our Buczacz and, although the honor was bestowed upon him after the city was no longer a shtetl, we the survivors are proud to claim him as one of our own.

There were other distinguished families in our town. Lebish Glanzer, the Shterns, the Millers, and the Frenkels, for example, were among our Talmudic scholars and esteemed sages. Rabbi F. S. Willig and the learned Hebrew teachers, Drs. Fernhof and Kofler, were also members of our community. Other, more contemporary figures include Dr. F. Nacht, a great secular scholar, Dr. Emmanuel Ringelblum, a historian who kept a chronicle of the Warsaw Ghetto existence, Simon Wiesenthal, the renowned Nazi hunter, and Dr. Marek Edelman, a Warsaw Ghetto fighter. Buczacz was also the birthplace of Sigmund Freud's father, although he later moved to Vienna. This was our aristocracy. We respected and admired these people, not only for their erudition but also for the way they modeled their lives according to the Ethics of the Fathers.

Dear old Buczacz—Jewish Buczacz—quiet dignity nourished its soul, and all parts of our community contributed to its vitality. Whether orthodox or assimilated, we were all Jews.

My father brought his family to Buczacz in the early 1930s. Prior to that, he had been the bachelor owner of sixty-eight acres of land in a village called Rustweczko, near Przemysl. When Anschel and Fraidel became Mr. and Mrs. Bauer, my father set out to build a new life. My sister, Bronia, was born a year after my parents wed, and a year and a half after that, my father was drafted into the Polish army to fight in World War I, defending Emperor Franz-Josef's Polish land against Russia.

In one of the battles, my father's army unit was completely destroyed but my father survived—the only soldier who did. When my father started to make his way to safety by crawling through the field of dead bodies, he suddenly saw two Russian officers approaching on horseback. Spying his movements in the field of the dead, the soldiers closed in on him—and my father said his prayers and prepared to die. "Are you gong to kill me?" Father asked the soldiers when he met them face to face. "No," they responded. "You did not fight because you wanted to; you had to by order of your emperor. You will go to a prisoner-of-war camp for a year, then you will go home." With his lips barely moving, Father said another prayer of gratitude to God. He was taken to Siberia.

Mother and the family had no news of Father for a long while. Then, after some months, a peasant woman came to my grandmother with the news that her son had seen Father, dead. There was no way to verify this information, so Mother and the family kept Father alive in their hearts. In reality, Father was practically free in Siberia. The conditions were agreeable and, because the camp was somewhere near the Chinese border, Father was once invited to dine at a Chinese home. "It was very good meat and vegetables," he told us children in his account of this meal, "but it was too fat." We laughed and teased *Tatko*, saying, "You ate Chinese pork, non-kosher food!"

When Father was finally able to get in touch with Mother, he assured her that he would be coming home after a year in the camp. But that year passed, and Father, Mother, and the family continued to wait. It would be six more years before Father could get on a ship home. Eventually, he sailed from Vladivostok and arrived home to the waiting arms of his wife and family. His daughter was not so welcoming, however. Crying hysterically, Bronia ran from this stranger, her father whom she had not seen in over six years.

But it was back to a new life. On his bachelor property, Father built a beautiful villa with a dining room, a salon, and a bedroom, all with attractive heating stoves with colored, glazed ceramic tiles from floor to ceiling. There was a large kitchen with a pantry and a wooden porch in the front of the house that led into a front parlor. Father eventually built a veranda, with colored glass windows at the side, and planted fruit trees in the back and on both sides of the house. The trees grew to become a large orchard of apple, pear, plum, cherry trees—and a walnut tree that grew to be a stately beauty. A sidewalk surrounded the outside of the house, and from it little paths led to a strawberry patch and a row of currants and gooseberries. Down from the house, on lower, flatter ground, Father rebuilt the old stable and a barn, renovated the well, and fenced off an area for a beehive colony. Ours was a small, picturesque, "sweet" home.

As the family grew—four more children over the years—Father sought to increase his income. He estimated his resources and planned to lease a larger estate. He owned the house and sixty-eight acres of land; selling all that, Father concluded, would allow him to realize his plans. His plans, however, were stymied when Jan Zelman, a villager of some stature, became interested in Father's property—and bought it. Soon, however, even before the sale was finalized, Zelman emigrated to the United States, to Chicago, Illinois, and left Walenty Misniak, the chief of the village, with full plenipotentiary power to handle and manage all matters pertaining to the property. After the down payment, the agreement called for future payments of $3,750 in American dollars, and the rest of the agreed price to be paid on a specific date: November 30, 1930. The payment was never made, however, so Mr. Misniak rented out the house, planted and harvested the fields, and managed the property in such a way that he realized a fine income for himself. At that time, there was a clause in Polish law stating that once a seller showed a buyer the boundary lines of the land, the buyer became the legal owner of that property. Father's demands for a settlement were ignored by both Mr. Zelman and Mr. Misniak.

The dispute then went to court, moved through years of trials, and eventually went as far as the state court in Lwów. Mr. Misniak intentionally stalled the proceedings by putting up stumbling blocks at each court session. After all, he knew that he had a good deal going for himself. Finally, on the eve of the War, Father won back the property, and I still have all the documents. Soon, of course, we were to lose the property—the Soviets nationalized it.

In the summer of 1937, when we were living in Buczacz, the Polish government gave all schoolchildren a vacation bonus: a child accompanied by an adult guardian could travel by train to anywhere in Poland without charge during the summer vacation. My sister took me to the train station and asked the first man she saw, "Would you kindly be a guardian to my little sister on the train to Lwów?" He agreed and so, attached to this guardian, I went to visit an aunt. I stayed for several days and was quite impressed by some of the things I saw in the big city: a gas stove, water that ran from faucets, flushing toilets—which amazed me the most—tall city buildings, and traffic lights. The human and vehicular traffic, the stores, and the window displays were all overwhelming; I did not hear one word of my aunt's tour-guide talk.

From Lwów I traveled to Rustweczko, to see our old "sweet" home and to visit my father's brother, uncle Aaron, and his family, who lived across from our old villa. One of Aaron's daughters, my cousin Leah, survived the War and we speak often about that particular visit. I could not go onto our old property, of course, because it was no longer legally ours, but I was able to visit the tenants of the house. I so much enjoyed climbing up into the attic and reaching out for the branches of the pear tree that produced a fruit that could only be described as "heavenly"; Father had planted only the best quality fruit trees. Leah remembers the pear juice dripping all over me; she was about fourteen years old at that time.

I recall the day she ran into the orchard without me, with a purpose unknown to me at the time. She was wearing a *dirndl*-dress, very much loved by young girls at that time. Such dresses were made of cotton print material, usually with red and pink roses on a green background. The dirndl had a full skirt and fitted bodice with puffed half-sleeves held in at the elbows by an elastic band. After a while, Leah appeared in front of me, her arms spread, her puffed sleeves stretched full. "Look!" she said, pulling apples from her sleeves like a magician. "They're yours! They're from your father's orchard!" I still laugh each time Leah describes this incident, to the delight of our families. Leah's son, Aaron, especially listens with avid interest to anything about the Bauers. He is the image of the Bauer brothers: tall, the same facial structure, the same posture, the same nature, and a handsome devil to boot—my favorite.

Father had surveyed several estates in counties of Eastern Poland and found one in Jósefówka, fourteen kilometers from Buczacz. By unwritten law in Western Poland in the 1930s, no estate could be sold or leased to Jews; this was not the case in Eastern Poland. Before we left for our eastern estate, however, the finances for a larger farm had to be considered, especially since the money from the sale of the small farm did not materialize. A partnership would provide a solution, so Father contacted a family in Moscisk that owned a flour mill. The brothers in that family lived in luxury, each one enjoying a comfortable life with his family. So good was their reputation, in fact, that the townspeople often deposited money in the safety of the brothers' homes, instead of in banks, for their daughters' dowries. One of these brothers became Father's partner in the new farm.

And so one sunny winter day, Anschel and Frieda Bauer and their children, Bronia, Monio, Etunia, Rumek, and Molus, arrived in their new home and settled on the estate, which had been leased from Jewish owners for nine years. The partner, Mr. Garben, settled in an apartment in Buczacz with his wife and two sons, and took a section in the manor house for his family, who visited occasionally.

As the years passed agreeably, Mr. Garben left the management of the farm to Father, as he passionately wanted to appear the "lord" of the estate. When he wasn't parading through the city in a *kareta* or a more sporty *bryczka,* he was galloping through the town and the fields—dressed in riding breeches and boots, whip in hand—astride a specially groomed horse. The "lord's" lifestyle, of course, was in great contrast to our own. While he engaged in evening entertainment and attended gatherings to play cards, paying little attention to the farm's business—except to keep a sharp eye on the finances—we struggled along as ordinary Jews, managing a farm to make a decent, honest living.

Soon enough though, disaster struck. The mortgage on the farm had to be paid. Now the mortgage on the farm was paid every year—on time—after the fields were harvested and the crop sold. One year, however, the money for the mortgage disappeared. When our partner was questioned, he gave lame, shady, stalling answers—and all the while, time was running short and the deadline for payment had to be met. If unable to make the payment, we would have to go to the poorhouse. We sent out appeals to our family: letters to my father's sister and my mother's father. Father's sister sent $400—but Grandfather saved the day, despite the fact that he was not a rich man. There was a transport of hay waiting to be shipped from our farm to Mother's sister in Rymanów, in Western Poland. Grandfather told Father to resell the hay and he would take the responsibility of offering an explanation to my mother's sister and her husband. We were saved by my grandfather's diplomacy.

When Grandfather Sholom Karpf came to visit us the first time, he came to unravel the intricacies of our family finances. I recall how my brothers and sister and I spent much time with him, clinging to him day and night and enjoying his loving embraces and playfulness. It was a treat for us to see Grandfather because his visits were so infrequent; he lived in Brzostek, near Rzeszów, which was a great distance from our town. I recall, too, listening to Grandfather leading serious discussions with one of us perched on his knee. How astonished I was to hear this Orthodox Jew, with his long beard, speaking a perfect, crisp Polish. As I mentioned earlier, in Eastern Poland the religious Jews spoke a good Ukrainian but not Polish.

After Grandfather helped us avert that near calamity, the farm business should have continued normally. Soon, however, perhaps only a week or two later, Father's partner suffered a heart attack and died—and more trouble ensued. Because Mrs. Garben had no idea what a farm was or how it operated, she turned to her lawyer and friends for advice. Now the farm provided us with a comfortable living but it was no "gold mine," as Mrs. Garben seemed to think. Although the original contract had provided for an equal partnership, there had been private items agreed upon between the partners when they formed the partnership—and for them, their word of honor had been enough. For example, Father's beehives and Mother's flower and vegetable gardens were to be exclusively and privately owned and cared for by Father and Mother. Mrs. Garben, however, wanted some portion of any profits Father and Mother realized from these small endeavors. Although it was ridiculous to bicker over such trivialities, the conflict was enough to cause the farm to eventually disintegrate. To live in peace, Father finally agreed to share the honey from his beehives with his deceased partner's wife, but she still demanded an increased income, partnership in the apiary, and more.

Father was deeply wounded by being suspected of dishonesty in these circumstances. My dearest father, for whom integrity and honesty were holy commandments that directed his life. He practiced *gemiloth chesed*, lending money but refusing interest. "Helping someone in need is a reward in itself," he taught us. Father would mediate, advise, or handle a transaction for a friend, taking no commission to which he might be entitled and simply wishing *mazel tov* (good luck) to the participants in the deal. He believed that there was a greater commission in the satisfying feeling one realized in doing a good deed for a fellow human being.

Lest I appear to be idolizing my father, let me balance my high regard for him with some criticism. The expression "he is good to a fault" summarized my father. I would say that Father's goodness of heart was innate, but his conception of humankind as respectable and trustworthy was faulty and to his disadvantage. Even before the War, every time some unscrupulous person took advantage of his kindness, Mother and Bronia just exchanged knowing glances, as if to say, "Yes, that is our Tatko."

My parents eventually left the farm when a new steward was hired, who literally ran the farm into the ground. About a year or two before the Soviets occupied Eastern Poland, the farm was rented to a Polish family, the Rosas, parents of Pani Blawadowa, a woman who later helped us during the Nazi years. The Soviets destroyed that family and demolished the farm; equipment and whatever else was usable were taken by the local peasants.

Under Soviet rule, we were glad to be off the farm and never claimed any connection with it. Obviously, the town was aware of our previous farm tenancy, as that was a common way to make a living. With some help from Bronia's friends, however, we were not placed on the list for Siberia. Meanwhile, Father's far-off "bachelor" farm, near Przemysl, was nationalized.

I remember the day "Lady" Garben shuffled over to the fence in front of our house in the city and begged for Father's forgiveness. Hitler was in power by that time, conditions were deteriorating, and her "friends" had abandoned her; they could milk no more benefits from her. I will never forget how the tears streamed down her face. "Please forgive me for my wrongdoing to you. I was ignorant and followed whatever advice they gave me. Now those good friends of mine have left me, and I am lost. Help me, please." Not for a split-second did we doubt that Father would not only forgive her but also help her if he could. Later, this same woman would send us a note begging us for a hiding place.

The estate in Jósefówka was a large farm, about eight hundred acres. The manor house sat amid gardens and an orchard—so huge that the end of it could not be seen when it was in full bloom—and the stables, barns, granary, and carpenter/black-smith shops were strategically spaced on the periphery of the property. A short distance behind these were the houses of the steady farm help. On the other side of the road, opposite the manor house, were the house of the head steward and the cottages of the dairyman, the cattle-barns keeper, and the foreman of the work force. Nestled just beyond our pond, less than a quarter kilometer away, was the little hamlet of Jósefówka, from which our estate took its name.

The estate was our home base, but a house in Buczacz was our second home during the school year. Father and Mother re-mained on the farm while my three brothers and I lived in the city, under the care of our adult sister, Bronia, so we could be educated in the city schools. Although Bronia had finished her formal education, she continued with various private lessons for personal enrichment and pleasure: violin, Esperanto, and German poetry. Her German studies were especially pleasurable, for the professor, Herr Landau, was a true scholar. More than once our rascally younger twin brothers were slapped by Bronia for mim-icking him.

In the last year of peace, Bronia and my twin brother, Monio, began to teach themselves new languages—she French, he En-glish. (Monio had studied French at school.) Bronia also painted and sketched. She did a portrait of Marshall Pilsudski, premier of Poland. When she sent the sketch to him, she actually received a thank-you letter in response. In later years, Bronia learned pho-tography and developed her own negatives; I still have those pho-tos. She also had a lovely voice, and I remember how her songs reverberated throughout the house, especially while we lived in the country home.

With all of her intellectual and aesthetic activity, Bronia still had the time to take good care of us. She was an efficient, orga-nized person and a strict disciplinarian. She was firm but loving—and energetically, fiercely, protective. As youngsters, of course, we resented the "boss" in her, and many a time came the rebel-lious cry, "I'll tell Mommy!" But after Mother died in 1938, we realized what a tender "mother" we had in Bronia—and what a loving and beautiful daughter she was to our father.

Although Bronia was probably twenty-six or twenty-seven years old at this time, her age was never revealed to us youngsters, and her "old maid" status was only whispered about. Nevertheless, she had an elegant social life in a club of academic friends; I have a picture of that group.

Bronia did have a few admirers and expressed varying degrees of interest in each of them. For example, there was David Blum, the music teacher. If the opinion of my family was all that mattered, David was a "great" musician. When they—Bronia, Monio, and David—would "saw those violins," the house echoed with their marvelous melodies. David was of the intellectual class.

Before David there was a high school teacher, B. Klahr, who wrote poetry for Bronia. He wasn't as "qualified" as David, though; David's writing was more sophisticated. I saved writing from each of them; a short Polish poem of B. Klahr and a letter David wrote in Esperanto. Sadly, B. Klahr perished in Siberia and David died in Lwów, a victim of Hitler. When our mother died in Lwów, before the War, David was there with Bronia and Father.

Bronia was also interested in a lawyer from Trembowla, a city in a neighboring district. When Mother died, and war broke out shortly thereafter, Bronia's interest in the young lawyer dwindled.

But friendships contribute to the pleasures of life, and there was another man that Bronia came to love dearly—as dearly as a brother. It started shortly before the War, when Bronia took a job as a bookkeeper at the Fillenbaum & Pohorile hardware firm. This alone created a sensation in town, for daughters of comfortable families simply did not work. Only merchant's daughters worked, and then only in their family businesses; most gimnazjum-educated women, like Bronia, did not "work." Of course, there were independent seamstresses, secretaries, and office clerks among the working class. In fact, I recall that Bronia had a friend—from a respected family—who lived with her elderly mother on the income from a meager pension but who, nevertheless, clung to aspirations to Jewish nobility. She would come to visit us, always in one of the two decent dresses she owned and wearing the same hat, gloves, and shoes. We would welcome her warmly and enjoyed watching her relish the light lunches we always shared with her. It was clear that she found these visits especially pleasant.

The hardware store where Bronia worked stocked construction and farm equipment, and most of the customers were peasants. The integrity of the bosses and their reputation for fairness made the firm a pleasant place to work. Yehoshua was the firm's head clerk; he had managed the store since it first opened and actually was more efficient than the owners. Everyone loved Sheeyka, as the peasants nicknamed him, and preferred to deal only with him. Sheeyka was tall and lanky, with a face that wasn't exactly handsome—yet he was a beautiful person. His blue eyes radiated intelligence, and he was honest and upright; he was a gentle soul and had a great sense of humor.

When the Soviets took over our part of Poland, both Jewish and Christian stores quickly went out of business. When the hardware store closed, Sheeyka got a job in a cooperative *soyuz*, and my sister joined him. We children could not wait for Sheeyka's Shabbos afternoon visits, those rare days when he was free during the short period before the War and under the Soviets. We would rock with laughter at his stories, jokes, and observations of human frailties. He was a learned Jew, well-versed in the sacred texts, and his quotations from the Bible and commentaries on specific stories were a joy to hear. He lived with his mother and two of his sister's children from the village, who attended city schools.

Bronia greatly enjoyed Sheeyka's company and the two were often seen together, which created yet another sensation and got the word "mésalliance" circulating among Bronia's friends. First it was her "working girl" status and then her relationship with a store clerk—when she was an educated girl with her *matura-gimnazjum* diploma. It did not bother Bronia, however, and we continued to enjoy Sheeyka's visits. I recall one happy afternoon, after Sheeyka left, I heard Father murmur, "*A guter, Yiddisher mensch,*" meaning "a good soul, an upright, Jewish-oriented man." It was a general observation addressed to all of us but, with a glance at Bronia, he was obviously hinting that she seriously consider this good man as a potential husband. Ever so gently, in case the remark seemed a bit dictatorial, and to assuage even a nuance of harshness in his intended meaning, Father added some

humor: "So what if he does not read Mickiewicz [Poland's great-
est poet]? He reads the Gemura [part of the Talmud] instead.
Sheeyka is a fine, worthy man." He obviously believed that
studying the Gemura put a man in the ranks of scholars.

Sheeyka spoke perfect Ukrainian and only broken Polish, and
he did not have a secular orientation. His literacy in the Hebrew
sacred texts was admirable, and his comments on politics, trade,
commerce, sports, Jewish history, Jewish newspaper articles, and
chapters from the Torah were all in Yiddish and, when spiced
with humor, they were especially stimulating and interesting. He
had not been touched, however, by the enlightenment of the
modern world.

Bronia loved Sheeyka dearly as a friend—we all did—and the
friendship continued until Hitler wiped out his family. Only
Sheeyka's niece survived and later emigrated to the United States.

Father's murmur about the "guter mensch" had a great influ-
ence on me years later. When I met Jechiel, the man who would
eventually become my husband, I had mixed feelings about the
relationship because the situation was similar to what Bronia experienced with Sheeyka. Jechiel did not get a chance to complete
his schooling as a youngster, although he tried to make up for it
as an adult in Jewish schools and Zionist clubs after World War I.
He spoke good Ukrainian and broken Polish, much like Sheeyka.
He was bright, had a sharp mind, a good sense of humor, and
strength of character; he was comfortable in the modern world
and was a caring and gentle soul. In my mind, I "detected" my
deceased parents' approval of Jechiel and appreciated the comments that "Grandmother" Hirschorn, a woman who would become a kind mother to us, offered about his family's history. She
stressed the family's respectability and decorum as well as its upright character—and this was enough for me. I felt like I would
be honoring my parents with a "guter mensch." In the Jewish
community, there was a kind of understanding that, as much as
the character of a marriage candidate was important, so was the
background of the candidate's family. But this is Bronia's story, so
I return now to the rest of the family.

We attended school six days a week and rushed to Tarbut Hebrew
school every afternoon to learn modern Hebrew. After these

classes, the boys went to Talmud-Torah/Cheder to learn Torah in biblical Hebrew. On the way from one school to the other, the boys often managed to squeeze in a small soccer game. When it made them late for class, of course, they had to bear the rabbi's scolding, but they felt it worthwhile. They also kicked the life out of their shoes on a regular basis, and that brought forth distressed but resigned sighs of reproach from Mother or Bronia. Schooling finished around six each evening, the higher Hebrew classes at seven; and then, after supper, study began anew—homework. Variously scheduled, Monio fitted in his now-and-then tutoring. Sunday, after morning Hebrew and our homework, was for recreation.

Monio, my twin brother, was an average student in the lower grades, but after he failed a subject in the fifth grade, he became a "genius"; he received straight A's and awards all through gimnazjum. He also joined Bronia in her violin lessons—without the benefit of prior instruction. He just began to play. To the surprise of the teacher, he picked up at Bronia's level, and she had been playing for over a year. Monio was brilliant in all subjects and excelled in mathematics and Latin. In fact, Professor Korngutt, his Latin teacher, often suggested that other students go to Monio for tutoring; "Go to the Doctor of Latin," he would tell them. Monio had the same proficiency in the Polish language, but his teacher graded him a notch lower. When confronted with this injustice she, in a cultured voice and with anti-Semitic acidity, retorted, "No Jew could master the Polish language to the level of an A grade." Monio was graduated, nonetheless, with highest honors and awards.

The younger boys, identical twins, were fun-loving A students but not scholars. They did their assigned homework and nothing more: no scholarly research, no readings, no extra-credit work. When it came to memorizing a long poem, for example—and this was a frequent requirement—they divided the piece and each memorized half of it. When the teacher called on one of them to recite, regardless of which one, the twin who knew that part of the poem stood up and recited. If, several pupils later, the teacher happened to call on the other twin and the stanza happened to be in the same section, the same twin stood up and continued. They even managed to switch if one's verse overflowed into the other's part—and the teacher never caught on. It was the same with everyone in town; no one ever knew which was which or who did what.

The twins were high-spirited youngsters with a lively sense of humor and, for good measure, they were handsome. I recall a crying/laughing episode when they were about thirteen years old. This was after Mother had died and we all shared in household chores. My specific chore was to wash the kitchen floor. One day I fell sick and I took to bed with a fever. The boys, Rumek and Molus, washed the floor. They did a good job and I praised them for it. As they came to the end boards of the kitchen, though, they placed the pail on the threshold, which was slightly raised. Wiping the floor and backing up toward the door, they tripped the pail—and the whole floor was flooded. At first we all gasped in shock, but then hilarity erupted as the boys slipped and slid in their attempts to stop the tide.

Throughout the school year, we studied, did our chores, and played in the city of Buczacz. During holidays, any school recess, and the eagerly anticipated summer vacation, we left the city for our country estate, Jósefówka. During those times, Father and Mother hovered about, attended to their chores, and enjoyed having the family together in one nest. Because we saw our parents only once or twice a week during the school year, we were always so glad to be home; we missed our parents. When we were together, we behaved like typical youngsters, of course, and were a nuisance much of the time. Truly, our reprimands or scoldings were deserved but, with our parents' love so evident, they did not hurt. Our feelings of homesickness and longing, so strong in town, were always wiped away once we arrived home.

In this affectionate environment, we felt carefree and happy, especially during our summer vacations from school. A typical day started early, at dawn. My three brothers and I—aged ten and under—would jump out of bed rubbing our eyes, run to the front door, squint, yawn, and welcome the glorious sunrise. Each of us in an old nightshirt, we would squeeze and push one another— "Let me in," "Don't push," "Move a little"—and sit on the threshold, delighting in the marvel of the bright ball peeking through the trees. That orange disk, that golden sun, climbing above the treetops and entering regally into the heavens, never ceased being a joy to us. The first soft rays of that "golden goddess" of the dawn would call us to a new day and awaken us to life.

Then heavenly perfume would drift in from the rose garden and soon the "game of breathing" began. Each one of us would draw in that intoxicating rose fragrance with deeper and longer breaths. Before long, the dogs would appear, and we would feed them as they frolicked with a noise that would awake or annoy Bronia—and thus the morning became a new day.

We would eventually get around to asking ourselves, "What shall we do today?" Because there were plenty of options, this was no easy decision. First thing in the morning, picking fresh roses was a must—that was an order from the kitchen. These were special roses that would be made into jam. This was a pleasant task and we willingly obliged. Not so, however, with the cherry or raspberry picking. Those luscious, plump, sweet cherries or raspberry "bubbles" were so edible, so tempting. To get a full basket, Mother would have to send kitchen help along with us. Capering in the orchard was a daily activity.

Sometimes we would make chocolate bars. After a great deal of hectic and hilarious activity in preparing the batter, amid squeals of delight and childhood laughter, we would pour soupy chocolate into our mouths from the matchbox molds. "Delicious!" we would cry with a glee that was clearly displayed on our faces—and clothes.

Exploring the farm's every nook and corner by ourselves or with Father was a day's recreation, and often there would be a soccer game in the afternoon; I would be the *bramkarz* (goalkeeper). But harvest time at the threshing machine was the most exciting. The din, the clamor, the workers feeding the machine at one end, a mass of grain cascading down at the other—all were marvelous. We would not miss that tumultuous activity. How happily childish we were—or perhaps we were just happy, as children are meant to be.

All this pastoral peace and contentment ended in the autumn of 1938, when Mother died after a long illness at the age of forty-six. She fasted on Tisha b'Av—a day commemorating the destruction of our ancient Temple—and had the usual "break-the-fast" meal. The next day, she woke up with cramps and a fever, and we suspected that a cucumber she had eaten after the fast was giving her the stomach ache. Doctors began visiting, then more doctors, until there were thirteen, twice a day, alternating the days. Together they diagnosed the illness as typhus, and each gave different treatment instructions. After four weeks, Mother did seem to feel better. Then, a week or two later, her leg suddenly started swelling, from thigh to toe, which left the doctors at a complete loss. Mother simply lingered on; some days she seemed better, some days worse. Eventually, the doctors ordered us to begin following some of their new ideas for relief. Father, Bronia, and I remained at Mother's bedside, attending to her needs night and day—but we were deluding ourselves.

Mother simply did not get well. When we finally faced that fact, Father arranged for Mother to see a specialist in Lwów, over the objections of the other doctors. Bronia and Father attended her on the trip, but it was too late. Mother died in the Lwów hospital, inhaling the venomous air of anti-Semitism during her last days.

The nurses at the hospital, products of anti-Semitic teaching, needed no lessons from Hitler; they abused Mother in their own way. Their greeting each morning was, *"Jeszcze zyjesz ty stara krowa, parszywa Zydówka, jeszcze nie zdechlas?"* which translates, "Still alive, you old cow, mangy Jewess. You didn't die yet?" And to add to the insult, they used the Polish word *zdechlas*, referring to the slaughter of animals, to become carrion. One day, after suffering the usual hostile greeting, and with fear eating at the fragile thread of her life, Mother begged Father, "Take me out of this hell"—her weak voice barely audible. The surgeon, Professor Ostrowski, a tender and beautiful person, could only look on helplessly at the nurses' shameful behavior. Although arrangements for a transfer were made, Mother died a day before they could be effected.

My dear mother! She was a beautiful woman. In fact, she was so beautiful that Father fell in love with her at first sight when they met. He was in the army, stationed in her town near Kraków, in Western Poland. His home was in a village near Przemysl, in Eastern Poland. When he announced to his parents his intentions to marry his beloved and asked them to put the matchmaking machinery into motion, their first question was, "How much is the dowry?" When Father quoted the amount, he received a firm, displeased response: "Not enough!" When the *shadchen* began negotiations, he actually had an easy job of it, for Father whispered to him, "Agree to whatever is offered; I'll make up the difference." So, in the spring of 1912, Anschel and Frieda became Mr. and Mrs. Bauer; they built a villa for their home, gave birth to five children, and lived happily—until 1938.

Mother loved her children dearly, maintained a warm home and, with her innate intelligence, oversaw their education. She often stayed with us in the city when Bronia would go to the farm. After her work was done, she would sit beside us with a book in her hands—she read voraciously—and would watch us do our homework. I often marveled at her profile, and my eyes followed the waves of her shiny black hair tied neatly in a bun. She often had to calm our disorder as we elbowed one another for space at the table full of books. Still, when we ran into the house, excited because there was no school the next day, she would sigh and laugh and say, *"Oy vey is mir."* "Oh, woe is me."

We were normal teenagers, of course, and had the usual dis-agreements among ourselves, with Bronia, or even with Mother, but problems were always ironed out. Although she attended us lovingly, Mother did not hesitate to administer mild punishments for infractions of household rules. She reared us to follow a moral code, her motto being, *"Zu Gott und zu Leute"* ("to God and humanity"). Although she enjoyed modern dress and environ-ment, she kept the Mosaic laws properly observed.

At Mother's death, our heartbreak could not be assuaged. Father, fifty-seven years old, grieved quietly and quickly became an old man. Bronia was inconsolable, reliving Mother's deathbed scene and bewailing Mother's suffering and death. My twin brother and I were sixteen years old; the "children," the younger twins, were not yet bar mitzvahed—not quite thirteen. Yet, we all grew up overnight and became "parents" in our own ways. For example, I attended to caring for both Father and Bronia, but Bronia needed special attention and I nearly had to force-feed her. I "bossed" her around, talked and cried with her, made her get dressed each day, and lured her to the kitchen to improve or save something I had spoiled—on purpose; all this to draw her out of her melancholy. But she would spring to life only in emergencies, always in defense of the family.

At the time of my mother's death, I was a student in the Jewish gimnazjum, founded by the Jewish community out of necessity. Beginning in the 1930s, as anti-Semitism intensified, the number of Jewish students in the municipal gimnazjum steadily diminished. Only a paltry number had been accepted into that school and, by 1937, only five students received that privilege, my brother Monio among them. The year before the War, only one Jewish student (Dziunek Frenkel, a friend of my younger brothers) was allowed to enter. My younger brothers, although they passed the exams, were not accepted. It is probably safe to assume—as the townsfolk did—that this one boy was admitted only because his mother, a math teacher in public school, had connections with a math professor named Hönig, who taught in the gimnazjum.

As the Jewish community observed what was happening through the years—the Jewish youth being barred from the halls of learning—it began serious and animated discussions about how it might remedy the situation. A decision was made and, by 1937, professors and distinguished members of the Jewish community organized a Jewish gimnazjum on the first floor of a large, modern structure—the Warszylewicz building. Standing four stories high, it occupied a full city block and stood as a prominent structure, with alternating pink and cream colors distinguishing each floor. With Jewish and Christian professors providing excellent instruction in literature, languages, history, math, and other secondary-level subjects, the school thrived.

Although I passed the entrance exams for the municipal gimnazjum, along with many other Jewish boys and girls, none of us were admitted. After the exams, some of us compared our test results with the Christian students' results, only to find that their scores were lower than ours, yet they were accepted and we were disregarded. It was obvious: the doors of the municipal gimnazjum were closed to us because we were Jews. Only the five Jews with the highest scores, Monio among them, were accepted.

I studied diligently in the Jewish gimnazjum and earned good grades, but I was not the scholar my twin was—and I resented the ease with which he grasped things. Fortunately, when I needed help in algebra I could turn to him, the "mathematician," for help. But Monio structured his time carefully, with activities scheduled to the minute, even social outings, and it was sometimes hard for him to fit me in. Although I ironed his shirts for him after Mother's death, he re-ironed them to meet his own standard of perfection. I was jealous and resentful of Monio, and became greater "friends" with my younger brothers: typical teenage behavior. In spite of it all, my twin brother and I were devoted to each other.

As a child, I spent most of my time with my brothers, whether we were on the farm or in the city. We played games and read together, and I especially enjoyed sketching trees and flowers. When we were in the city, we enjoyed the Skalki Beach on the River Strypa, where we would gather with our friends to go swimming, fishing, and boating. I recall one day when my friend Lusia and I, along with a Ukrainian girl named Kataryna (a farm girl who had been accepted at the gimnazjum and boarded with a neighbor), went for a boat ride. As we glided pleasantly and smoothly along, suddenly, we felt ourselves being drawn toward churning waters. As Lusia and I worked frantically to control the boat, Kataryna panicked. When a boat of young Christian boys came sailing past, Kataryna called out, "Stop, take me with you! Let the Zydówki [Jewesses] do what they will." Lusia and I bitterly vented our anger by splashing our oars so as to soak Kataryna, and then safely steered the boat to shore.

Our years in public school involved a great deal of reading, writing, and arithmetic—serious work—plus recreational activities. I myself spent a lot of time sketching, painting, and scribbling. When the geography teacher asked me to paint scenes for each province of the country, I decorated one entire classroom wall with my landscapes. I also drew a portrait of Maimonides (a Jewish philosopher who was born in Spain in 1135 and who served as a physician to the court in Egypt) for our religion class. Yes, we had religion classes in a state school; Polish and Ukrainian priests came to teach the Christian students, and Jewish scholars taught the Jewish students. Ours was actually a class in Jewish history, and when we studied Maimonides, Professor Kriegel put my portrait of him on the desk. Although it was called a "religion class," prayers and holidays, Bible, and Hebrew language were excluded. For this, we attended Hebrew school in the afternoon.

I also have pleasant memories of our excursions to the forest on Lag b'Omer—a minor holiday, celebrating Bar-Kochba's heroism. (Bar-Kochba was the leader of the Jews in a revolt against Rome in Judea in C.E. 132–135. He liberated Jerusalem and minted coins to commemorate the date of the city's liberation. Although he was killed in a later battle, he remained a folk hero to the Jewish people.) Also memorable are the Hebrew language shows we gave in the Sokół theater center, celebrating holidays, Purim Spiel, or Chanukah. As I remember those days, all the joys and sorrows come back to life.

3

Two Years of Soviet Occupation

HITLER INVADED POLAND on September 1, 1939, and all the "problems" the Poles had with the Jews were resolved in the years to come; Poland was divided between Germany and the Soviet Union. Hitler had conquered the western two thirds and Stalin had seized Eastern Poland, from the San River in the south to the border of Lithuania in the north. Buczacz came under Soviet occupation.

In the first days of the occupation, the Soviet soldiers were bewildered by the fully stocked stores and ran from one to another, buying up whatever they saw: boots, clothes, cosmetics, textiles, lingerie, wristwatches—their arms were covered with watches, from wrist to elbow. The items most eagerly sought were boots, watches, and women's nightgowns, which were sent to their wives and girlfriends.

As soon as the new government established itself, various departments were created to control the town's affairs. Shops, warehouses, residential buildings, and farms were either nationalized or heavily taxed—which resulted in great losses to the owners—and soyuz cooperatives were created to sell groceries and other consumer goods. Officially, one church and one small Jewish prayer house were allowed to remain open, primarily for show. The rest, the Great Synagogue, the Klasztor Cloister, and the Hebrew schools were closed. Other schools were open, but lessons were given in the Russian language, from handwritten pages, not books. Native Russian teachers were brought in from Russia, and Polish teachers had to take crash courses in Russian.

Every able-bodied person worked for a minimal salary, barely enough to buy a loaf of bread once a week. This resulted in a lot of business for the black market, of course, and many people ended up in prison for privately buying and selling goods and services. Many Soviet officials also shared in the black-market profits.

In the early weeks of the occupation, people from both towns and villages, Polish and Jewish alike, were deported to Siberia. The Soviets arrested the *kulaks* (rich farmers), rich business people, Polish officials, military men, and the Polish aristocracy. They, their families, and refugees from Western Poland were sent deep into Russia. As Hitler's army drove through Poland in 1939, many Jewish families fled into the eastern part of the country ahead of his forces—only to find themselves under the control of the Soviets.

Among these refugees was our father's sister, her family, and her daughter's family. Once they escaped from Hitler's forces as they advanced on Przeworsk in the West, the group headed to Moscisk, which was in Eastern Poland and, therefore, under Soviet rule. After the exile of the "enemy"—the rich and patriotic native Polish citizenry—to Siberia, life began to quiet down for a while. Then one day, an order was issued for all refugees to come to the municipal offices to register for return, if they wished, to their homes in Western Poland. Most of them, of course, wanted to return. They felt so forlorn, so stranded, that they wished to be in their own homeland, their own towns. The night after registration, all the refugees—along with any remaining "enemies"—were pulled from their beds, loaded into trucks, and sent to Yakutsk in Siberia. My father's sister perished there, but her family survived.

Under the Soviet regime, life changed for everyone as privileges and rights were curtailed and comforts greatly diminished. For Jews, at least life went on, and no matter how harsh things might be, life was not as bad as the hell Hitler would soon put them through. Although they might be arrested for being late to work, for stealing a lump of coal from an office bin, or for any number of crimes real or fabricated, at least they could walk the streets legally and not in fear of death.

Our family lived quietly. Bronia earned a small income, and Father managed to support us by exchanging items from our home for cash, by bartering for food, and perhaps by a little bit of black-marketeering.

Then, in June 1941, Hitler violated the Molotov-Ribbentrop non-aggression pact with Stalin by sending his troops into Eastern Poland and, from there, across the borders of the Soviet Union.

II

NAZI INVASION

They hunt our steps,
that we cannot go in our broad places;
our end is near . . .
To our very necks we are pursued. . . .

Lamentations 4:18

The Nazis March In: Early Atrocities

AFTER THE SOVIETS FLED, the Germans entered Buczacz on July 5, 1941. On that day the roadways, windows, balconies, doorways, and sidewalks were filled with people. watching the German forces as they marched into town. The Ukrainian population was wild, of course, and welcomed the troops joyously. War machinery rolled in and happy German soldiers marched briskly, one after another, winking and waving at girls all along the way. This was a river of killing materiel, human and metal monsters, flooding the region. Depending on the eye, or rather the heart, of the beholder, it was a vision of glory or gloom. As I watched in a kind of rigid stupefaction, it felt as if we Jews were watching an avalanche bearing down upon us, one that we could not escape. Although the day was sunny, we felt a pall of fear spreading in the air.

In a small secluded recess in the side of a house, huddled with other Jewish children—all of us low-spirited—I stood and watched the future marching in on us. I recall how we turned to one another and asked, "What will they do to us?" and "Is it true they are so bad?" Of course we had heard of Hitler's pronouncements and the rage he vented upon the Jews, but all that had been sketchy gossip, hard to believe—or perhaps we didn't want to believe it.

We began getting answers to our questions within the week, when Jews started to become the targets for a kind of "free-for-all" behavior. Beat a Jew, rob a Jew, make sport of a Jew, kill a Jew; it didn't matter. Savagery reigned. While the Ukrainians acted on their freedom to do whatever they liked to a Jew, the Poles, a minority in our region, remained stunned and guarded.

One day, during that first week under Nazi rule, I was standing in line at a bakery when several Ukrainian thugs suddenly took control of the crowd. As a Jew neared the entrance of the bakery, the Ukrainians maneuvered themselves into position and prevented his entrance. A commotion broke out, which, of course, was the whole purpose of their action: to create an opportunity to beat Jews and deprive them of bread. Emotionally hurt, and many of us physically harmed, we scattered in different directions.

Another day the Germans, along with several Ukrainians, provided amusement for the Polish and Ukrainian population by ordering three bearded Jews—two middle-aged and one elderly—to walk into a shallow part of the river. Before shoving them into the water, the SS men took great delight in shearing off the men's beards. Then, from the bridge above, they commanded the Jews to perform various outrageous and exhausting gymnastics, to the delight of the spectators, of course.

In the beginning, all such incidents were mere entertainment, but when the Nazis got to the serious business of the destruction of Jews, they set to it with German precision. First they called for representatives of the Jewish community, to whom they presented their demands. The prewar Jewish Community Council, the Kehillah, became the Judenrat. Just as it had managed Jewish affairs before the War, it now had to speak for all Jews and "deliver" on the Nazi demands.

The first order was for all Jews to wear the yellow Jewish star on a band around the arm. Then came the orders for Jews to relinquish their gold and furs; delivery of these treasures was set for a certain date, and failure to comply meant the penalty of death. The everyday drafting of craftsmen and able-bodied men to work also began in these early days. Women, too, had to report to the marketplace, where they were assigned housework at Gestapo headquarters, homes, offices, and the like. All this was followed by various restrictions: For example, entrance to public facilities was forbidden; trading, shopkeeping, and searching for food were curbed; a curfew completed our imprisonment.

Then came the ackjas. As soon as we had one, rumors of another being imminent would begin to circulate. Any news, bad or rarely good, would electrify the town, and Jews would rush to one another to gasp out the news of a new decree, a new demand, and a harsher restriction. All the news clandestinely acquired came from the Judenrat. Its building, in the center of town near the Great Synagogue, was the center of bustling activity. Mendel Reich, prewar president of the Kehillah, was the first to preside over the Judenrat, followed by Baruch Kramer and then B. Engelberg. These men were highly respected and displayed great integrity. The managers, men named Kanner, Berger, Sterner, and others, whose positions did not last long as they fell in the akcjas, were responsible for several "departments," taking care of various affairs and problems that beset the Jews. On a daily basis, the *arbeitsamt* employment office had to deliver workers to the quarry, fields, and shops; it also had to arrange for large detachments to work at demolishing Jewish stores. They were responsible for getting women to clean the apartments and offices of the Gestapo; for managing the orphanage, which was filled with the poor, the sick, and lost children following each akcja; and for seeing that the soup kitchen had the supplies it needed.

Management of the Jewish police was an onerous responsibility, especially controlling them so that they would behave humanely to their brothers. They functioned in an atmosphere of irritability, despair, and depression. The worst and most enervating situation developed when the Gestapo ordered the Judenrat to provide a specified amount of human cargo for transport to Borki Camp; if the quota of victims was not filled in the roundups, the Judenrat had to decide "who shall live and who shall die" and deliver the required number of men. Understandably, this led to painful conflicts of conscience and caused terrible and tragic discord within the Jewish leadership; their task was maddening and executed in despair. In frustration, the presidents of the Judenrat and other officials kept changing their posts. Some were themselves caught in roundups; others, at the end of hope, resigned from office or, more drastically, from life itself. One of the later presidents, B. Engelberg, a gentle and noble person, resigned and attempted suicide. Eventually, he was killed in an akcja.

The previous reference to the Jewish police needs clarification, because there are conflicting records regarding the behavior of that force of Jewish men—of the conduct of a police force in a time that promised no tomorrows.

Some men—teenagers, students, and older men—joined the force as an opportunity to better their existence. Some of them were of rather low moral character to begin with, and perhaps others sank lower with their circumstances, all of them thought, erroneously, that they would save their lives by serving the enemy. I recall that the policemen who came to our house to call for my brothers, who had defected from the demolition work unit, were students and not at all rude. In the three calls that they made, they never entered the house; rather, they stood at the doorway while Father, Bronia, and I, or whoever happened to be at home at the time, gave excuses. "They went to work this morning but they mentioned something yesterday about having to report to another work unit" or "They went to work this morning; they left before 7:00 so they must be there by now" or "They forgot their armbands."

The young policemen would accept our excuses and go away, leaving only a light admonishment for our brothers. According to a diary kept by Mr. J. Klonymus' brother, written in the grain fields of the outskirts of Buczacz, the Jewish police were all dark-alley characters, and it is true that many of them drove Jews out of their homes with excessive haste during akcjas. They would search zealously and pull their victims out of hideouts with un-necessary force. Understandably, they were detested and hated by those who witnessed their behavior. Did they have to work so efficiently? Their defense was that SS men were at their side, watching their performance, and if they did not do their jobs efficiently, they would be forced to join their victims. Sadly, they did their work well—and for their help in the liquidation of the Jews, the Nazis rewarded them with postponement of their own extermination.

In our city the younger adults in the Jewish police were the best of the lot. They performed their jobs like robots, although they did attempt to be decent. Occasionally, they were the ones who signaled to the community that an akcja was about to hap-pen—but there were many false alarms. Nevertheless, villainy and cowardice overshadowed the humane spark in some and forever disgraced the name of the Jewish police who served the Nazis.

5

The First Rejestracja

MONIO, the eldest of my brothers and freshly graduated from the gimnazjum, had been assigned to work in the quarry. Together with other Jews of various ages, he performed full days of hard labor under the whips of SS men and the Ukrainian police. Then, on August 25, 1941, the Gestapo ordered a "registration"; all men aged eighteen to fifty had to appear at the police station to register no later than 6:00 that evening—and the penalty for absence was death. Monio returned from the quarry all dusty, sweaty, and breathless, grabbed something to eat, and rushed off to the police station—and that was the last we saw of him. Four hundred and fifty men, including Monio, were shot in the forest on Fedor Hill in the early morning hours of August 26, 1941.

This was the first massacre in our city. History has recorded the event in a summary paragraph, compressed into two or three lines, much as I have described above. I have seen television documentaries and read documents from Yad VaShem: lists containing dates, events, and cold dry facts. Can you visualize a father, confined to a house by the curfew, listening for hours to a barrage of machine-gun shots from a nearby hill, instinctively feeling the shot that felled his son, and dying with him emotionally? No two lines can contain or express the anguish in our Jewish homes at that time. Perhaps Eduard Munch's painting "The Scream" can offer some inkling of what it felt like. The impact of this tragedy left a numbing grief in every Jewish heart.

I find myself thinking that perhaps in the early evening hours Monio did not understand that he was in the jaws of death. But as imprisonment dragged on into the night, deadly fear surely must have crept into his soul, as well as into the souls of all the prisoners. They no doubt speculated aloud about sharply increased oppression and harsher persecution—but not death.

"You can't imagine how we felt," one of the survivors told us later. "Our suspicions: What would happen to us? Why were we there? Our desperate calculations: a mixture of dread, hope against hope, fear for our families and, at the same time, fear and anger under the abuse of the Ukrainian police." The men debated among themselves during their long hours of waiting. They imagined scenarios and vaguely predicted their future: there would be a rash of new decrees for them to carry out, harsher labor on a special project, stricter discipline—a mean future, but still a future. It did not occur to any of them that they would be murdered.

Although this was the beginning of Nazi atrocities on a grand scale, none of us believed that they would slaughter innocent people. Not until we were staring into the barrels of our murderers' guns did we realize how wrong we had been. To our horror, Hitler's followers, the elite SS—*Sturm* Commandos (Gestapo units specifically trained in cruelty)—soon convinced us otherwise. They and their Ukrainian and Polish accomplices committed murder—murder of Jews—with a zeal that far exceeded "duty" and that betrayed their obvious enjoyment of it all. On that fateful August day, our Nazi masters selected their victims carefully. Students, lawyers, merchants, doctors, office clerks, professionals, and the Jewish intelligentsia were of no use to the German system and could be eliminated. While Monio was among the new crop of graduates and was thus selected, craftsmen and other healthy laborers were spared, only to be utilized to exhaustion and ultimately "liquidated." The men selected for execution were imprisoned overnight, while the vicious Ukrainian police kept an iron watch over them and beat them at the slightest pretext.

At home, imprisoned by the curfew, my family and I were filled with worry as evening stretched into night and Monio did not return. At about midnight we saw our eighteen-year-old next-door neighbor—a schoolmate turned policeman—arrive home for a quick meal. We grew up with this boy and often helped him with his schoolwork. Yet, this neighbor, this "policeman," hurried by us and would tell us nothing; he simply waved us away with a gruff remark and a look of disgust. His "work" left him sweaty and boisterous, and his wild eyes glistened with sadism. We fell back, aghast and defeated.

So my brother's agony might have been the prospect of living hell, which actually began right there, but not thoughts of imminent death. As the Ukrainian cruelty increased with the night, however, some of the men must have realized the truth. Others, no doubt, forced themselves to hope for that special *arbeit*, and kept themselves fooled. All were shackled by fear, besieged and helpless. Then, at 3:00 in the morning, the Gestapo and their willing accomplices, the Ukrainian police, sprang to their task. They herded, shoved, and terrorized the frightened mass of men up the Fedor Hill, into the Sosenki Forest, where their rhythmic machine-gun fusillades destroyed the wishful thinking of the victims with an awful and brutal finality.

Those must have been long, infinite minutes of dumb and paralyzing fear. The men were lined up in groups of about twenty and the machines of death went rattling. Next . . . next . . . next. . . . Again . . . again . . . again.

I still hear that terrible sound of chilling thunder—I will not, I cannot, ever forget it. Each volley of shots from the hill bombarded our hearts and set our every muscle vibrating with pain. Father, ashen, clutching his heart while sliding to the floor, brought out his sorrow in rending, sobbing moans. Our arms around one another, we were a grieving cluster of humanity, fighting the sounds of death while still resisting the belief that murder was being committed. But the roar from the hill persisted, irrefutably confirming the truth. Our sorrow was later deepened by reports circulated by eyewitnesses: the killers themselves! In coarse, jocular tones, the gloating Ukrainian police proceeded to describe specific episodes during their "work." I recall hearing about how one young Jew did not wait for regrouping and ran down the hill—only to be shot instantly for "disobeying orders."

The sounds of firing long echoed in the city, striking ghastly fear into Jewish hearts and creating a new perspective for us, a new sensation of being locked in a cage and set on fire.

6

Struggling in the Cage

WE CONTINUED OUR STRUGGLE for existence. With conditions deteriorating day by day—new orders, new demands, and new restrictions that made our lives increasingly difficult—we began to fear the approaching winter. Because it was forbidden to help Jews with food supplies, black-market prices skyrocketed and Jews began selling their clothes, linens, and household items for food. As our misery grew, the peasantry thronged to the city on market day and, together with the burghers, hunted for "good buys" of Jewish goods. With time, as our desperation deepened, their greed turned to shameless lust. A coat bought a kilo of potatoes or less. With the help of our peasant servants from the village, who would bring us small bundles of potatoes, flour, and the like, my family managed. Of course, we thanked them with presents. In the early days, if it were possible, they were glad to have a rest stop and a cup of tea. I recall the time when a Ukrainian policeman caught them in the act of bringing us a can of milk—he actually saw them from the street above—but by the time he tore into the house, we had been able to hide it. He was furious but, having no proof, left us with only a threat.

Those who had the means managed to secure food during the early months of the Nazi regime, but the prewar poor and the Jewish refugees from Hitler's Germany who had fled to our city were cruelly stricken. The Judenrat extended as much help as they possibly could to those people, of course, and the town's Jewish families also tried to share their meager meals with these destitute. But with each depressing day, the German refugees found themselves even more despondent. They were stranded and desperate. In 1941, as Hitler marched further east and occupied the eastern part of Poland, pushing the Soviets out, even more refugees from Germany flooded our region—running away from Hitler, away from persecution. Some returned to families but most were strangers to the area. For a while a German Jewish family stayed with us. They were piously Orthodox and had three small children, one only a baby. They were gentle, modest people, utterly bewildered in their desolation. Many others, along with their children, came with little more than the clothes on their backs. They sold what few possessions they had, even ripping a jacket off their bodies so as to secure a pitcher of milk for a baby. The meager soup kitchen established by the Judenrat for the helpless poor also gave them some support. But a bigger problem than supplying food was how to shield them from the akcjas. After all, they were strangers lost in a foreign town; where could they seek cover? They knew no farmer and no friend in the Christian community to whom they could appeal. Space in crowded, tiny holes in cellars or attics was limited and usually built only for family groups. Yet, they were taken into hiding by the town's Jews. Sadly, many perished, together with their protectors, as one family—for in life-or-death situations we unite; we are one Jewish family.

I will not forget the fate of two more refugees: Wolf and Shaye Karpf (my mother's twin brothers). They lived in Frankfurt am Main in Germany and, on *Kristallnacht* ("The Night of the Broken Glass," November 9, 1938), were severely beaten. Shaye surmounted his aches and, with some difficulty, surreptitiously transported Wolf back to Brzostek, to their parents' home. Wolf died of his wounds shortly thereafter, his parents at his bedside. Shaye reached Palestine, physically and emotionally injured, where he lasted only a few short years.

And so the Jews, whether natives in their town or refugees, were all helpless and in despair. There were many such desperate people in our city. I recall a tailor, his wife, and their three young children who lived in a basement cave in our courtyard for some years before the War. All consumptive scarecrows, they were starving even before the War. During that time, the Kehillah was helping take care of these sick and indigent people. With time, however, due to the circumstances, the Kehillah could help only on a much reduced scale. I recall how Izio, the family's youngest child, a boy of about four, would visit us daily because he knew that we adored him. He had an angelic face, features chiseled to perfection, and large blue eyes fringed by black eyelashes—we loved that face, and he was a dear child. Little Izio would come up to see us every day, sitting somewhere in a corner and quietly watching our every move. He would glance at the table, at the stove, especially at a dish with food in it, but he never asked for anything to eat. Father, Bronia, or any of us would feed him whatever was available at the moment, and Bronia would hold him on to her knees and try to coax him to smile. She delighted in his every word and motion, and constantly looked at him as if to try to solve the mystery of why such darling, beauteous innocence should be destroyed. It was incomprehensible to her—humans causing humans pain and suffering. Her humane, sensitive soul could not reconcile itself to the sorry reality. Under the Nazi occupation, the family had become walking ghosts. Their lot was one of unspeakable misery. Eventually, Izio and his family were among the first to be taken on the transport to the Belzec death camp.

Pani (Mrs.) Bienerowa also lived in our backyard. She was an eighty-year-old widow who was poor and lived on a meager Polish government pension. Before the War and through the Soviet years, Mrs. Bienerowa came to us every evening and spent a pleasant time with my parents. After Mother died, she would come by to have tea with Bronia and Father. She was a highly educated lady and spoke perfect German, Polish and, of course, Ukrainian; she quoted much German and Polish literature and often sprinkled it with Latin. She was an aristocratic woman and stimulated many of our discussions. I remember how my siblings and I would do our homework at the table while the adult voices floated toward us. Sometimes we even became involved in the conversations—with an ulterior motive, of course; we valued Mrs. Bienerowa's advice in solving some of our homework problems. And, although we appreciated the help, we were reluctant when it was time to escort her home at 10:00 at night. Each of us squirmed at the prospect, and we would alternate the nights, dreading the cold weather. I recall how Monio, especially, was irritated by the interruption to his studies.

When Hitler's forces came to Poland, Mrs. Bienerowa's daughter and son-in-law in Kraków were killed, and Mrs. Bienerowa was utterly wretched. A distant niece took her into her room, where the conditions in that congested Jewish section were miserable. It was so bitter, in fact, that Mrs. Bienerowa, with the future appearing bleaker each day and her hunger increasing, left her crowded accommodations, went to the marketplace near the ratusz, sat on a bench, and waited—for death. It was the only way she could relieve her suffering, and it soon appeared that her wish would be granted when a Gestapo officer arrived and began to question her. His interrogatory tone soon changed into a conversational one when he heard her speak; her beautiful German intrigued him. Nonetheless, Mrs. Bienerowa spoke bluntly and honestly about her philosophy on the civilized German nation turned uncivilized—she always spoke her mind quite plainly. In this instance, of course, there was no doubt what her purpose was: she wanted to deliberately provoke the man and, in the end, she was successful. The affronted officer pulled out his revolver and shot her on the spot, in plain sight, in front of witnesses.

7

Forced Labor: Release for Ransom

MY FAMILY got through the winter. All men were conscripted to daily work and the Judenrat weekly assigned various jobs to women. My brothers Rumek and Molus worked on the demolition of a row of Jewish stores, but Father was over the working age. Bronia's and my turn came in spring 1942, when we were assigned to work in the Trybuchowce Camp and in the farm fields. Our group of women worked under the direction of a Jewish foreman who reported to the Ukrainian police who, in turn, were supervised by the Germans. Our lunch consisted of a cup of milk. In the evening we arrived home with the boys, who would be returning from their demolition work, and fell into Tatko's (Daddy's) arms, pressing and kissing him to assure ourselves that we had him and he had us—and that another day had gone by and we were still together.

Then the day came when not everyone returned home. Our two *kinder*—we always called the youngest two the "children"—were caught in a raid to form part of a group slated to go to the infamous Borki labor camp. I recall that when the first transport of men was shipped to Borki, we in the community knew very little about it. After the next roundup and shipment of men to the camp, the Judenrat arranged with the Gestapo to provide wagons so we could send food packages to our men there every two weeks. The food was provided by the families, with some support from the Judenrat. The wagoneers brought back very sad news: Borki was a hard labor camp where the men were worked and starved to death and, periodically, executed. In these miserable conditions, men who were not killed for a "crime" would collapse from exhaustion. Even though men sent back messages or regards to their families with each transport of food, after a few weeks in the camp, a man's messages would cease—and we could only imagine what had happened to him. Our neighbor's daughter, Leika, experienced this. She made a special trip to town from her place of hiding with us to send packages to her brother at Borki. But she did not have to collect and pack the food for long, for after he was in the camp a short while, Leika stopped hearing from him. As for whether the food ever reached the prisoners, we will never know.

Before transporting each group, the Germans kept the men imprisoned for four or five days and let it be known that releases were possible and could be bought. They knew that this information would provide them an ideal opportunity to squeeze out all possible valuables from the Jews. Furs and gold had already been confiscated, but the Germans surmised, correctly, that there must be "leftovers" somewhere. When a bribe was paid, a prisoner was released.

When our brothers were detained for transport to Borki, Father took out the jewelry we had: Mother's watch on a gold chain that had wound twice around her neck, reaching below the waist; Mother's ring with a cluster of good-sized diamonds; Father's own exquisite gold watch on a gold chain; and one hundred zlotys. With these valuables, Father proposed to buy back his own children, and Bronia took them to an intermediary to handle the deal. It took days, with rumors circulating that each day was the last to buy freedom. These rumors were spread purposely, of course, to maintain the pressure for bribes. The Jews milled around the prison, watching, spying, listening to everybody and everything, with the Gentile onlookers enjoying the whole show. One day Bronia got near the barred prison window and saw our brothers. With deep sadness in their eyes, they called to her, *"Broniu, ratuj nas! Ratuj nas!"* ("Save us, rescue us!"). Our older brother, Monio, had already been trapped and killed. With that memory, and the feeling that the same fate was awaiting them, they were a picture of fright and despair.

Distraught with heartbreak and frustration, Bronia ran home. "No! No!" she cried, "it mustn't happen. It can't happen again! Why? Why? Oh, God!" While she began pressing the intermediaries, urging them to act more forcefully, I returned to the prison, myself, anxious for a glimpse of the children. I was standing there

deep in depression, absorbed in bitter thoughts, oblivious to the
world, when suddenly I heard, *"Weg, du verfluchte Jude, weg!"*
("Beat it, you damned Jew, scat!"), and a fiery slap on my cheek
and ear sent an electric shock through my body. I flew from the
Gestapo officer like one possessed but, when I reached a safe distance and was able to catch my breath, I realized what hilarity I
had provided for the public. The mob milling around observing
the Jews' sorrow had seen the Nazi spring upon me without
warning. Judging from the resounding laughter I heard in the
distance, the scene must have been most entertaining.

It took days to free the "hostages" because of the constant hag-
gling between the Gestapo and others down the chain of negotia-
tors. The loot collected by the intermediaries was supposedly
going to the Gestapo, but not all of it did. For example, we gave
the money and the jewelry to a neighbor, a Ukrainian woman
married into a Polish family, and she contacted a Ukrainian friend,
Wisiakniewski, who was a man of consequence in the Ukrainian
community, as well as a friend of the Gestapo—and we prayed in
a fever of hope. After several days, again pressing the woman for
results, Bronia and I stood in the street by the prison and saw
Wisiakniewski talking to the Gestapo, discreetly pulling out only
Father's pocket watch and chain. Within a short while our boys
were in our arms. The rest of the loot that we had provided for
their ransom remained with our "friends."

With that near disaster, we promised—vowed—never to let the
boys get caught again. We blocked off a small room with a wardrobe, settled the boys in there, and never let them go to work
again. Although the Jewish police came calling for the boys several times, we were able to keep the children hidden and thus
protected by telling fabricated stories.

The sad thing was, of course, that the fate of those without the
means to bribe was sealed. This inequity was commented upon,
and there was a great deal of grumbling: "The rich buy their
freedom and the poor take their place." This particular roundup
of men for Borki took place in spring 1942.

8

It's Going to Happen. It's Tonight. It's Tomorrow: A Harassed Existence

SUMMER CAME—and nothing had changed; we were constantly hungry and afraid. Every day brought a new crisis; we called them "heart attacks." I recall one Friday night, as we celebrated a semblance of a festive Shabbos dinner, with little food but candles burning, a neighbor burst in with news that an *oblawa* was beginning. We left everything, ran into the corn patch down by the river, and hid there for about two hours. Fortunately, it was a false alarm. Had it been an actual raid, the corn patch would have been a worthless place to hide from expert hunters. Such "heart attack" experiences were frequent, mostly in the early evening or late at night.

In the meantime, my brothers remained in hiding. We had rescued them from being shipped to the Borki labor camp by "buying" them back with jewelry and money. Determined to prevent a repeat of the raid and their imprisonment, we kept them in that miserable cubicle of a room, all shaded and blocked off from the world; we had no choice. Street raids became more frequent and more brutal, and the Jewish police were far from polite in their inquiring and spying.

Father remained at home while Bronia and I went to work on the farm-estate of Gaje. Bronia was acquainted with the director of that estate and arranged a job for us—and as long as we presented work papers to the Judenrat, it was legitimate work. We took Leika with us and picked tomatoes, acres of them. It's no surprise that the first two days we ate more than we picked, for the tomatoes, plump and juicy, were a delicacy to three hungry girls. After a few days, however, we atoned for the sin of stealing by experiencing a severe cleansing of our systems. Although we were able to put aside some of the tomatoes, along with whatever else we could find to take home—a few potatoes, a beet, an apple, and some wood for fire—we simply could not look at another tomato. Because the surveillance of the police and the SS men made it hard to smuggle anything back to town, we used side streets and alleys, which took more time and made reaching home before curfew an added worry.

Every day, while oppression of the Jewish population increased, our lives deteriorated and disease, hunger, and general desperation claimed the weak. With uncertain tomorrows and mounting dreadful rumors, our fear increased. Without even referring to the dreaded event by name, "It's going to happen" and "It's tonight!" became formidable phrases. The threat and suffocating fear of the ever-impending oblawa invaded and dominated every facet of our taut lives.

I recall the evening that we were shocked to find Rumek and Molus covered, face and body, with a rash of large sores. They were pale and gaunt, and we understood that their pallor and the rash were the result of a lack of air and sun—and that the real culprit, which caused a vitamin deficiency, was meager food. We started letting them out of their hiding place at night whenever possible, sometimes during the day, and trying to provide them with better food. Eventually, their bodies healed, but their spirits, like those of us all, kept plunging lower. Father, having lost his eldest son, was trembling with fear for the fate of the rest of us. He aged visibly, day by day, as he thought about our conditions, the overall Jewish situation, and the foreboding future. As we watched that gentle, beloved face, overwhelmed by sorrow, our own emotions, a mixture of sorrow, frustration, and love, became almost unbearable.

Bronia organized and managed our household. We kept working on the farm through the summer, while Father remained at home with the hidden boys. We returned home every evening, grateful to find them still there, each day a gift of life. All the while, rumors of an impending pogrom circulated and grew to a frightening, maddening pitch, leaving us tormented, harassed, and completely shattered by the signals of a coming massacre. At any time, day or night, a neighbor might rush in, hysterical, with "It's tonight!" or "It's going to happen!" or "Tomorrow!" Living this way made our existence feverish and frayed our nerves to shreds. In the autumn of 1942, when the danger loomed ever closer, we arranged with one of our peasant friends to hide Father and the boys until it passed. In the meantime, Bronia and I worked on the farm by day and kept guard at home by night.

Home from work one night, Bronia and I were falling asleep in our clothes, thinking of Father and the boys in the village, when a neighbor broke in, breathless, eyes bulging with fright. The dreaded phrase was not necessary. Along with the Issakovers and their five-year-old son, we ran—but where? We did not know. To the forest? Maybe. Grateful for the pitch-black night, we ran to the Strypa River where we stole a small boat and crossed to the other side, rowing carefully to minimize the sound of the oars moving through the water. Passing through a few orchards, we reached a steep point of the Fedor Hill. Invigorated with the confidence that we had made a successful escape, we reached the top of the hill, descended on the other side, pressed on into the forest, then again onto the riverbank, for one of the S loops of the river surrounded the hill. We reached a deep part of the woods and remained there for two and a half days. Fortunately, we had brought some food with us and were clothed well enough to handle the chilly air. But the real chill we felt was in our hearts.

In the solitude of the forest, with time to think about our overall situation and with trees as our only friends and protectors, our depression deepened. Still, we countered our gloom with unreasoning hope, but poor Mrs. Issakover, a young mother trying to comfort her child, bewailed its future. On the third day, when the terrifying sounds of animal noises helped us decide to return home, we inched toward the city, frightened even by the gentle flutter of a leaf. We arrived at dusk only to find that, once again, there had been a false alarm—one of many that continued to rob us of our stamina and sanity.

Long afterward, and to our horror, we learned that the spot we had passed, the clearing in the forest on the edge of the river, had become the killing field in later akcjas.

9

The First Akcja

THEN, SUDDENLY, it became real. Bronia, Leika, and I were returning home from work one day, about dusk, when we realized that the very air felt menacing. Jews were running in every direction because a large contingent of Gestapo, SS men, Ukrainian police, and Latvian police had been seen entering the city. It was known that the Latvians exceeded the Ukrainians in brutality and were brought in for akcjas because of their "efficiency."

This was October. The fields were bare, all harvested, but conical, tent-like clusters of corn stalks had been left to dry in certain sections. We each crept into one of those "teepees" and sat there through the excruciatingly cold night—and none of us had coats or sweaters. Although the days were still sunny enough for a light dress, a night on the bare soil was bitterly cold. I sat on my hands, warming them one at a time in my armpits. It was impossible to stretch, so with my knees bent, I kept switching the contact of my backside with the icy ground, from one buttock to another. I was numb and stiff and cold—and so were Bronia and Leika. Later, I wondered why we didn't, in the darkness of the night, step out and move around a little to try to warm up. No doubt, fright kept us just as frozen as the cold night air. So great was our terror, in fact, that we didn't make a sound even to one another throughout the long night.

At dawn, when we peeked out to see how to prepare ourselves for the day, we were appalled at what we saw. The fields were swarming with frantic Jews, running, gesticulating, generally behaving like escapees from an insane asylum. We came out of our shelters and met them with inquiries, but no explanation was really needed—and besides, they were incoherent. They were gasping, and the fright on their faces told all.

Not knowing where to go, we simply followed the crowd. Even peasants—two old women, in particular—were moved, stopping us with "*Yezus Christus!* Don't . . . *don't* go to the city! Have mercy, Lord! It's a slaughterhouse!" We ran deep into the forest's underbrush, collapsed, and huddled there for three more days, just the three of us—we had broken away from the rest. We sustained ourselves with the tomatoes in our pockets, a few apples, and a piece of bread that had been given to us by a kind Uzbekistani-Soviet soldier, prisoner of the Germans, who worked at the farm. Fortunately, it was warmer in the forest than in the open fields. The sun occasionally penetrated the treetops and, even though the nights were cold, they were bearable when we rested on a bed of leaves in the low undergrowth.

The sight of those terror-driven Jews stayed with us, and our sorrowful thoughts were with our people in the city. Leika cried herself to sleep, for her parents and two sisters were there as well; her brother had already been taken to the Borki labor camp. Our hearts were heavy with worry over her impending tragedy, but as for our own loved ones, we felt a measure of relief. Father and our brothers were, we hoped, safe in the village in a farmer's barn.

On the third day, searching for signs of safety, we cautiously ventured out of the woods and slowly reached the city. There, the scene that assailed our eyes and hearts was . . . what words can describe the wicked works of a demonic power? Horrid sights that will stay in my memory forever! Violated Jewish homes, rows of shattered houses, gaping holes instead of windows, smashed doors, dangling balconies, bloody walls, bloody streets. At every turn we saw more destruction. Shambles of pots, dishes, everything strewn all over, down bedding ripped open and the street white with feathers, clothing flapping on a staircase, a lost bundle, an overturned slop pail, a dried puddle of blood, a child's shoe. Ghastly, ghostly sights.

Because we entered at the west end, we had to make our way through the entire town to reach our home. As we walked through the residue left by that hurricane of raging madness, we could not speak. Something pushed from inside our beings and choked us, so that words could not free themselves from our morass of sorrow. Dumb, blind with tears, but still seeing what was to be seen—the inconceivably tragic reality—we reached our street, our houses. Our home was turned inside out, but we were too overwhelmed with grateful thoughts that our dear Tatko and the children had escaped that fury.

Not so for Leika; her family had been wiped out. The landlady reported that Leika's old father, crippled mother, and two sisters had run in their nightgowns into the closest vegetable patch by the river, only to be pulled from their hiding place, forced to the railroad station, and shoved into the waiting cattle wagons.

After the massacre we knew that Father would be looking for a sign that would reassure him that we were alive, so for two days we watched the road and the farm wagons passing by. Finally, we saw a few familiar faces: Father's protector-farmer and his son. Not wanting to attract attention to them or ourselves by having a conversation, Bronia and I followed discreetly behind them. In the crowded market, while buying potatoes, we were able to whisper to them, "It's quiet now. Let's bring Father and the boys home."

No words were spoken at our reunion; nothing could be said to express our emotions. We simply fell onto one another, into one body, our souls talking. The moment Father saw Leika, he said, "We cannot leave her, an orphan, alone." From then on, she lived with us, and we took her along into hiding.

This was the first akcja in Buczacz: October 17, 1942. (The August mass murder had been called the first rejestracja.) Over fifteen hundred Jews were packed into railroad cattle wagons and sent off to an unknown destination. With time, vague rumors spread that the Jews had been transported to Belzec. In their elemental drunken madness, the killers murdered the feeble, the sick, and those who resisted; about three hundred Jews were taunted, beaten, and shot on the spot. The survivors of the akcja, those who saw the murders or heard the screams from their concealment, reported these facts, but the condition of the bodies left on the streets and in the homes made their own testimonies. The Christian townspeople, not at all reluctant observers, witnessed these sadistic atrocities and gossiped about them.

Waiting for "It's going to happen!" and "It's tonight!" and "It's tomorrow!" became a constant torment, destroying even the most levelheaded, strong-minded people. The persistent fear of being caught in an akcja increasingly tortured us. The fear of being shot for a "crime" or at the whim of a Jew-hunter, the general fear of death at every step, combined with hunger, disease, and all our other misery, was devouring every Jew.

Meanwhile, the Nazi plan to create a ghetto was becoming a reality. With news traveling at lightning speed, it soon became obvious that crowding us into a confined area would certainly facilitate the roundups. The proposed ghetto, or "Jewish quarter," was to be Podhajecka Street, 3-Ciego Maja, Grunwaldzka Street, and part of the Bashty, a deprived, poor section of the city. Slowly, Jews were expelled from their homes in surrounding villages—Jazłowce, Koropce, Monasterzyska, Potokztoly—and brought into Buczacz, into the ghetto. In spite of the loss of thousands of Buczacz Jews in the akcjas, the flood of those Jews from the surrounding villages overcrowded the Jewish households, and the frantic, anxious activity of the poor, desolate, refugees was heartbreaking.

While the Judenrat established a soup kitchen and tried to help settle the new people, Buczacz Jews were naturally affected by the situation. When Bronia and I went out to survey some of the streets and houses in the Jewish quarter, where we would soon be forced to settle, we found dismal conditions. "But we'll have to move somewhere!" we said to ourselves, so we reluctantly chose a room in a house on Grunwaldzka Street. At the time, however, we weren't sure that would be a good place and had hoped to return to decide for sure.

When Bronia and I went home and talked to Father about what we'd found, our conversation was filled with anxiety and dejection. Suddenly we asked ourselves, "What are we going to do with the boys? They have to be hidden"—and the accumulated irritation and fear burst from our hearts. No, we were not going to fetter ourselves with shackles, not voluntarily. We decided, instead, to leave the city and go into hiding. We did not know what the future held, but we felt and hoped it would be better. Father made arrangements with a farmer friend, Mr. Orsiawski, for a corner in the attic of a barn and, in a highly agitated state, we made our preparation to flee Buczacz.

For years, we had been friendly with our Ukrainian next-door neighbors, the Karkewicz family. Mr. Karkewicz was a railroad official and Mrs. Karkewicz was our landlady; they had two sons and two daughters. Our mother had always been ready with advice and help for the older daughter, who had a lovely infant. The son-in-law was a fierce Ukrainian nationalist and had been imprisoned by the Polish government. The younger son had been our classmate and needed much tutoring, which we provided, but he became a policeman—a beastly one at that—the one who would not speak to us on the fateful night of the first rejestracja. Our families were friends in peacetime and, although it seemed we would remain friends when the Ukrainians gained power in the administration of the city, the warmth was noticeably gone.

We gradually sold our personal possessions for food but, as our situation became more threatening each day, we distributed some remaining valuables—clothing, linens, silver—between our two Christian neighbors for safekeeping. Mrs. Karkewicz, the landlady, gladly agreed to store other valuable household articles for us, such as a sewing machine, dishes, furs, bicycles, rugs, kilims, rich velvet-embroidered bedspreads, bolts of dress fabric, and some small pieces of furniture. When we approached her about hiding all this in her cellar, before the akcjas began, the old friendship seemed to be renewed and her friendly smile told us, we thought, "The more, the better." When the time came to extract some things from the cellar to give to our other benefactors as "gifts" for our shelter, however, the woman had all kinds of excuses and protestations, such as, "It can't be pulled out of the overcrowded cellar." I particularly recall an argument over the sewing machine. Since she thought we would all be dead soon and our possessions would all be hers anyway, the woman's true colors emerged. We didn't get the sewing machine, but settled for what we could. As for the rest, the large wardrobes and such, they remained in our house and were ravaged in the akcja. The windows and doors barely closed, we left our home without even locking the door.

A week after we left our home, on November 27, 1942, a second akcja occurred. Twenty-five hundred Jews were hunted down, herded into cattle cars, and shipped to their deaths. Two hundred and fifty were killed in town. Although we were gone, the nightmare followed us.

The ghetto came into being late in 1942. Podhajecka Street was its center and each of its small rooms housed ten to twelve people. In other neighborhoods, Jews could occupy only the houses on the north side of the street, and a 5:00 P.M. curfew held occupants captive while police patrolled the streets.

Our Leika, who hid with us for a while, returned to the city and lived with her cousin in the ghetto. Later, she had much to tell me of life under those conditions. I especially recall one of her reports relating to the Jewish struggle to survive. Before we left the city, we understood—it was common knowledge—that the local population, both the city and the surrounding countryside, was hostile to Jews. During the akcjas, and especially when Buczacz became cleansed of Jews—Judenfrei—the most evil thugs surfaced and scoured the very depths of the city to seek out and denounce hidden Jews. The most notorious, cruel creature was a dog catcher named Nahayowski. He and his gang raked and ferreted out every bunker, every attic, every corner, every house, and denounced the Jews they found. After the ghetto's liquidation, Nahayowski still sniffed around, but for better results he turned to the suburbs and their vicinity. In our hiding place at Mrs. Blawadowa's, the youngsters from the Bresher family, who had escaped from the ghetto, gave us heartwarming news. A Jew, whose parents Nahayowski had delivered to the Gestapo, broke into Nahayowski's home at night and shot him dead. The news brightened our day.

III

IN HIDING

> For the enemy hath persecuted my soul;
>> he hath crushed my life down to the ground;
> he hath made me to dwell in dark places, as those
>> that have been long dead.
> And my spirit fainteth within me;
>> my heart within me is appalled.

Psalm 143:3–4

10

IN THE ORSIAWSKI CHICKEN COOP

UNDER COVER OF NIGHT, moving cautiously, stealthily, we arrived at Orsiawski's farm in Józefówka, a hamlet next to our former country estate which, except for the manor house, was now completely in ruins. Father, Bronia, the two boys, Leika, and I climbed up to the attic above the farmer's chicken coop and nestled into the straw. After our more than two–hour, anxiety-filled journey, and after the tormented year and a half in the city, we felt a sense of relief, as if we had been sick and our fever had broken. The feeling soon passed, however, and we knew that the sickness in our world was still with us and that our fever would soon return.

So began our struggle to live. Our efforts to survive were comparable to those of a person thrown into river rapids, floundering in raging waters, intermittently surfacing, gasping for air, but eventually drowning. That was to be our fate.

The Orsiawski family, in whose farm we found shelter, was a reasonably well-off, churchgoing, and respected Polish-Ukrainian household. The husband was Polish, his wife Ukrainian. He was a handsome man, who had been extremely happy to be friendly with Father, the master of the estate. Before the War, he had been eager to learn to read so that he might improve his social position. We children became his tutors. At many a lesson, after he had laboriously combined a few letters into syllables, we would be quietly amused to see the droplets of sweat that formed on his forehead. "It's easier to chop wood," he would say, laughing at himself. He was a good man.

His Ukrainian wife (his second wife), on the other hand, could have been the model for Cinderella's stepmother, as we found out too late. Although Father was friendly with the man, he usually greeted the woman only in passing; none of us knew her very well. The couple had six children; three teenage boys and a girl of about twelve—whom the woman worked to excess—were born of the farmer's first marriage. The two children of this union, a boy of ten and a girl of eight, were also required to work but had a much lighter burden. One could not help but notice the older daughter; she was a gorgeous girl and pleasantly good-natured.

For us, settled in the straw in the attic, life followed a limited routine. We sat, we slept—in our clothes, covered with our feather quilt—and we waited for food. At mid-morning we were given a pot of borscht with a bowl of potatoes. At dusk we received soup made of groats and greens mixed with diced potatoes, as well as one lump of bread to be shared among us. Eating in a semblance of peace made it tasty, however. We went to sleep each night only to awake each day to the same routine, grateful for the roof over our heads and what seemed to be safety.

Winter came—and cold winds and snow seeped through the rafters. Every morning the quilt was covered with frost and crackled with our every move. Eventually, the frost and snow would melt, then the quilt would be damp and cold; when the weather became bitter cold, the quilt remained stiff and frosty all day. Seeing Father's eyebrows and mustache glinting with frost every morning, which would have been amusing in a carefree time, was not a cheering sight.

We passed the hours of those winter days listening to the outside sounds. Sometimes the woman's scolding or pummeling of her stepchildren was all we heard. Because we could not move around or talk much, for fear that an unexpected neighbor or a playing child might overhear us, we communicated through gestures and whispers. When food came, usually brought by the children, but sometimes by Mr. or Mrs. Orsiawski, we encouraged conversation to learn anything that might give us hope.

As it became colder in our confining, cage-like attic, our overall situation seemed to become more straitened. Although our own circumstances saddened us, we pitied the people who remained in Buczacz. At least there were no SS men at the farm!

Then one day, an SS or Gestapo officer did appear in the yard, right next to our coop, but Mr. Orsiawski could not understand what the man wanted, nor could we; the man's German was muffled. The name "Bauer," however, did reach us, and this was enough to give us a bone-chilling scare. The reference was to "farmer," apparently, which is the translation of the German word *Bauer*.

After nearly five weeks in hiding, we felt increasingly hungry and realized that the borscht had become watery, the soups gradually diluted, and the potato portions skimpier. We also noticed that when the food was delivered by Mrs. Orsiawski, it was handed over brusquely, which told us that our "rent" was due—not actual rent, of course, but the intimation that all the goods and money we had advanced had been exhausted (or so our hostess evidently calculated). When we complied with the hinted request and handed over more money, Mr. Orsiawski, as a friend, was a little discomfited. Avoiding all eye contact, he would accept what we offered, probably out of fear of his wife's reaction if he didn't. We would try to ease his discomfort, probably created by pressure from his wife, by saying, "Well, after all, we have to eat."

I recall one market day when Bronia and Leika, bundled up in bulky peasant clothing and kerchiefs, went to the city with Mr. Orsiawski. Pulling out some items of value hidden at our Christian neighbor's home, Bronia loaded our farmer's sleigh and then he left; Bronia and Leika remained in the city. Leika had a chance to send a food package to her brother in Borki, and she needed time to collect the food and arrange for the parcel.

A day or two later, Bronia and Leika made a disastrous journey back to us on foot. Caught in a blizzard, driven by winds across huge drifts of snow, frozen to the bone, they stole into barns along the way for shelter. Some farmers let them warm up, most chased them viciously, and one especially murderous man chased them with dogs. They had to arrive at our hiding-place at night, of course, or at least at dusk, to avoid detection. After their fourteen-kilometer trek, they arrived thoroughly drained, frozen, frightened, and dejected, and they had dismal tales to tell, for the oppression of Jews in the city continued.

After paying our "rent" each time, it would seem that the quality of the food would improve for a while, then the game would be

replayed. For us, hungry and fearful, huddled together in the biting cold or fidgeting aimlessly in the straw, the days became long
and endless. I recall one time when we were eating I watched
Bronia take the spoon from the bowl; it contained only a speck
of potato, a speck that she chewed forever. In that moment I
realized that she was trying to leave more food for the rest of
us, and it broke my heart. I choked on both my potato and my
embarrassment—why hadn't I thought to do that?—and followed
her example. The boys were so hungry that they began stealing
eggs from the coop. Disposing of the shells was a problem, of
course; the "evidence" had to be buried, and that was difficult.
Then, too, a greater number of missing eggs would lead to discovery of the thieves, and we could not take that chance.

It became obvious to us that another trip to the city for more
goods was needed to remedy our food shortage. We were hungry
and cold, and our eyes relayed the messages our voices couldn't
speak. Dear Father, our *mensch*, who in peaceful days would attempt to remedy whatever was saddening even a stranger, was
now trying to make his own children believe that his hunger was
no discomfort to him. Often on Friday nights he brought an *oh-
ray-akh*, a guest, to the table, a poor Jew from the synagogue, to
share our Shabbos meal. To Father, this was a *mitzvah*; besides, his
good soul enjoyed the feeling of comforting someone. And those
hungry teenagers, Rumek and Molus! They would sigh just imagining the luxury of a whole loaf of bread. I recall how we would
curl up in the straw, listening to Father's *krishma*, the bedtime
prayer, quietly mumbling it along with him into the straw. Routinely, we would decide that Bronia and Leika needed to go to
the city on the next market day for more of our belongings, hidden with our neighbors, so that we could "pay" our hosts.

In this way, we persevered, endured the harsh conditions, remained always anxious—and survived the winter.

11

"I Felt 3,000 Bullets
Riddle My Brain"

DURING THE FREEZING WINTER of 1943, dismal news reached us
from the city. People were routinely denouncing hidden Jews—
their former neighbors—in the city and in the countryside and,
of course, the Nazis or the police murdered the betrayed Jews. As
word of this reached us, the constant agony of fear intensified.

Once again we needed to pacify our protectors, so Bronia went
to the city to get a substantial amount of clothing and household
articles, and to convert some of our possessions into cash to cover
a longer period of time. There she found the city in the grip of
typhus and a population of emaciated Jews wandering furtively,
seeking food, seeking help.

Bronia planned to spend the night in our abandoned house in
Buczacz and return to the farm the next day. At about midnight,
Leika, who was spending the night at her landlady's, learned from
the landlady's son, a policeman, of an imminent akcja. She ran to
Bronia and gasped, "It's tonight! It's really tonight! A policeman
told me! Run! Run wherever you can! I can't go with you, I
must run to tell my cousin!" (After hiding with us for several
months, Leika had left to remain in the city where she could
prepare packages for her brother in the Borki labor camp.)

Bronia seized her jacket and, not even lacing her shoes, ran in
the direction of our village—but police blocked the end of the
street. With her heart in her mouth, she turned to run in the
opposite direction, to the farm where we worked in the summer.
She had to go through the center of town. Although the streets
were deserted and she crept in the shadows, through small streets
and alleys, she eventually had to cross the very street and pass the
very building that housed Gestapo headquarters; there was no
other way. Consumed with terror, Bronia literally crawled on all

fours, in the shadows, crouching and sliding along the walls. Following a few more back streets, she finally reached the castle on the hill and, from its ruins, she descended into a mostly Christian neighborhood and continued to the countryside. She reached a barn, frozen with fright, frozen with cold, and utterly exhausted, but the warm stable corner was heaven to her.

In the morning a Uzbekistani farm worker, a war prisoner of the Germans who knew Bronia from her work that summer on the farm, was sadly surprised and very moved when he found Bronia shivering and frightened. He cried and confessed that he, too, lived in fear of the Nazis. "I am like Jewish! We don't eat pork." He made her a bed under a trough, among the cows, and filled the hidden space with straw. He then brought her warm milk, bread, and cheese, for which she blessed him.

Bronia cherished her safety, but as she heard the stable boys at work during the day talk of the fleeing Jews in the surrounding fields, her feelings of security lessened and fear increased. At a safe moment, her protector came to the stable and confirmed that, indeed, Jews were scattered everywhere in the surrounding fields. Still worse, the farm's utility storage building, directly across from the farmhouse, was filled to suffocating capacity with Jews. In his opinion, the danger was great; he was sure they would be denounced and the farm would be searched. For her own safety, he strongly advised Bronia to leave that night, and she did.

After the stable boys finished their work at the end of the day, without even waiting for the bread her protector would bring her, Bronia set out and walked toward the Ukrainian village of Zyznomierz, which was known to Jews as one of the most hostile villages in the vicinity. She had hoped to reach the home of a prewar family friend, the farm's director. She plodded through the snow and arrived at the farm late that night, feeling lucky to have found the right house given her struggle with both darkness and fear. Although the chained dog's fierce barking frightened her, she somehow managed to climb onto a fence, then to a barn roof, and onto the top of a pile of hay. She bored into that haystack, pulled hay over her head, and stayed there for what seemed like forever.

In the morning the director, who had heard his dog's barking during the night, came out and inspected the yard. When he noticed the disturbed layers of hay, he climbed to the top of the haystack, recognized Bronia, uttered only, "It's you?" and left. Bronia never saw him again. Neither he nor anyone from the house came near the haystack. We had come to consider not denouncing a Jew to be a good deed, and Bronia appreciated this as an actual favor.

Our city nestled in the loops of the S-shaped Strypa River that ran through it, with the suburbs and surrounding villages set on and around the riverbanks. The village of Zyznomierz, where Bronia hid in the haystack, was located directly across from the banks of the river on which the Nazis, on that particular day, carried out their largest mass murder of Buczacz Jews. It was later learned that several large pits had been prepared in secret on the banks of the river, in a forest clearing called Legi, and for two days—February 2 and February 3, 1943—the Nazi murderers, with the help of their ready and eager collaborators, Latvians and Ukrainians, dragged three thousand Jews, men, women and children, up the hill and down into the waiting ditches. There, with monstrous brutality, they killed the Jews with machine guns and then covered them with dirt, dead and wounded alike. The peasants reported that the River Strypa turned red as the enormous amount of blood from so many victims saturated the soil and seeped into the water. Two hundred fifty other Jews were killed in the city itself.

In tears, Bronia later described to us that daytime fusillade of machine guns. "Three thousand bullets riddled my head, and I felt every shot echo in my brain!" She sat there in her haystack and, for two whole days, the rhythm of the machine-gun fire pounded her head and heart. With that sound assaulting her crying soul, her heart sank, her strength ebbed away, and her only means of sustenance consisted of two lumps of sugar that she found in her pocket. Those two days of horror were emotionally devastating, and it seemed to Bronia that they would never end. Despondent, she drifted in and out of fainting spells, trying to keep herself conscious with handfuls of snow. When the sound of gunfire finally stopped, Bronia, feverish and stricken, prodded herself toward the city. There the incomprehensible sights and the ghostly appearance of the city following the akcja completed her emotional and physical exhaustion. She collapsed on the floor in the bare bedroom of the home we used to live in, the entire Jewish town having collapsed as well. Nothing can describe the devastation; the all-encompassing word *pogrom* only begins to approach it.

The news of the atrocities in the city quickly reached us at our attic in Józefówka, and we were crushed. Each day that Bronia did not return seemed to confirm for us that she had been caught in the slaughter and, when we looked at her empty spot in the straw, our grief only deepened. Father's sobs, mixed with broken, muffled murmurs of pain and prayer, would tear at our hearts, and any attempt by the boys and me to console our dear Tatko only made us all cry harder.

Then, about the fifth day, a ghost appeared—and I can barely describe our reunion; Bronia could not be seen from under the heap of our embracing bodies. But she was not the same—drained and exhausted, she could not breathe or talk, she could not eat or sleep. She could not live past the nightmare. Day after day, she remained sluggish and limp, dozing in jerky naps, sitting in a daze, or crying in fits and starts. Sobbing, she told us, in bits and pieces, of what she had heard, what she had seen. Her soul needed healing.

Bronia had been a strong person, physically and psychologically healthy. She was an organized person, very energetic, and often appeared strict, but that was only because of her high standards. In reality, Bronia's whole being felt deeply for her fellow human beings. She would share another's pain, and the need to help reduce that pain was imperative to her. And she had a boundless sense of devotion to family. My dearest Bronia! In my young teens I would resentfully ask her, "Why don't *you* do it?" when she told me to perform some chore. I never realized that she always did her utmost to do more than she needed to do.

Bronia never went to the city again, no matter what. We decided that we would simply pay our "rent" and debts after the War.

Map of Poland before World War II.

Above: Anschel
and Frieda Bauer,
c. 1910. *(Author's
collection)*. Right:
Anschel Bauer in
Austrian army,
c.1914. *(Author's
collection)*

Above: Frieda and Bronia Bauer, c. 1916. *(Author's collection).* Left: Bronia Bauer, 1937. *(Author's collection)*

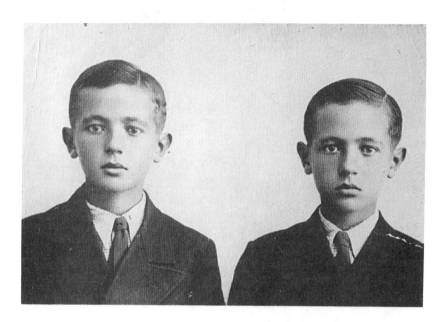

Above: Molus (left) and Rumek Bauer,
1938. *(Author's collection)*. Right:
Monio Bauer, 1939. *(Author's collection)*. Below: Bauer family, 1937.
(Author's collection).

Sholom and Pearl Karpf, author's maternal grandparents. *(Author's collection)*

Above: Wolf and Shaye Karpf, Frieda Bauer's twin
brothers, in Germany, c. 1925. *(Author's collection)*.
Below: Anschel Bauer's sister, Ronia Ringel, with oldest daughter, Erna. *(Author's collection)*

Above: Giza Shuldenfrei Dym,
author's cousin, c. 1920; refugee
from Hitler, survived in Siberia.
(Author's collection). Right: Leah
Bauer Singer, author's cousin,
1946; survived in hiding. *(Author's collection)*.

Above: Bronia Bauer, standing at left (in fur-collared coat) with her club friends, c. 1935. *(Author's collection).* Below: Strypa River flowing through "downtown" Buczacz, under the Gimnazjalna Bridge. On right, center building: the court, prison, and police station. Above, extreme right: Basyliany Klasztor. *(From "Sefer Buczacz." Used by permission of Zeev Anderman).*

Esperanto letter written to Bronia Bauer by a friend. *(Author's collection)*

Left: Ratusz (City Hall). *(From "Sefer Buczacz." Used by permission of Zeev Anderman).* Below: Wall of the Great Synagogue in Buczacz. *(From "Sefer Buczacz." Used by permission of Zeev Anderman)*

Bridge over Strypa River, leading to the girls' public school (on the left) and the Sokol Building on the right. The upper level of the Sokol was a theatre; the lower level was the library. *(From "Sefer Buczacz." Used by permission of Zeev Anderman)*

Buczacz survivors at a memorial service, c. 1945. Unveiling the monument for the Jewish victims of the Nazis in the akcja of February 2 and February 3, 1943. *(Author's collection)*

Julian Katz, 1947. *(Author's collection)*

Etunia Bauer Katz, 1947. *(Author's collection)*

12

A Quarrel

WEEKS PASSED, full of tension and worry. It was the end of March or early April 1943, and news of Jews being hunted and killed continued. This news somehow forced Bronia to emerge from the effects of the unforgettable horrors she had witnessed weeks earlier. With the fear of death hovering about us every minute, day and night, we kept to our attic and existed on watery borscht and shrinking potato portions. The boys risked stealing more eggs and a little chicken feed which, besides nourishment, offered the benefit of giving the boys a day's work, for they had to pick the kernels from the husks. Sometimes, however, they threw away the kernels and husks in angry frustration.

By this time, the peasants were growing tired of hiding Jews. Originally greedy for Jewish goods, they had calculated that filling their homes with Jewish spoils was worth the trouble of hiding Jews for a few weeks or months. But the War dragged on with no end in sight, and our suffering, our dying, grew to be of less and less concern to them. Hiding us "endlessly" *was* a bother, even though most of us gave some kind of "payment" in return for food and shelter. Those who were sincerely compassionate were few and far between.

I remember one evening, sometime in early April, we heard a commotion in the yard outside the barn. Mrs. Orsiawski, our "hostess," was quarreling with her husband's brother. They had become bitter enemies over the ownership of a six-inch border strip of inherited land. She claimed it was rightfully her husband's and, therefore, hers. As their quarrel escalated, we heard our names mentioned and we stiffened with fright over the inevitable consequences. Sure enough, after the fight subsided, Mrs. Orsiawski ran to us and, still fuming, said, "You must leave. He knows you are here, and I am afraid the neighbors heard it all."

We had to go, but where? With her "You must leave, hurry!" ringing in our ears, with shoes in hand, coats hastily thrown on, carrying a bag with our paltry possessions—a knife, some toiletries, and our treasured *siddur*—we ran. Where? Just out into the open fields. Conscious of our father's delicate health, we had always taken special care of him, but now I could not keep from crying at the sorry sight of Tatko running barefoot in the cold, damp grass.

We tramped through the fields, a bewildered, frightened, and utterly forlorn group. Unexpectedly, we came across a lonely structure in the field. Even though it was still in the village, it was a distance away from the cottages and would serve as shelter and cover for a while. A tiny hut, it had a bench along one wall that probably provided a resting place for weary workers. Although there were several square feet of free space, we climbed onto the bench to get into the hut's attic, with Father, the tallest, helping us up. Then, just as he placed his foot on the bench and grabbed the edge of the opening to pull himself up as well, he suddenly started groaning and gasping, his eyes bulging with pain. We froze in horror, thinking that someone had followed us in and was stabbing or beating Father from below. We simply did not know why he was in pain and, when we tried to help him, we only caused him more agony. Finally we realized what had happened; the opening through which we had climbed was a small air vent, too small for a man of Father's size. With great pain, he maneuvered his body and managed to ease himself up into the attic with the rest of us. We dressed his ugly abrasions as best we could and then huddled together for the rest of the night in the tiny attic space.

We stayed there over a week. Bronia went to our former protector's cousin, a widow named Helka, for some food and information about the quarrel that had forced our departure. Yushko, the brother, asked to meet us. "Miss," he said to Bronia, "I would never, never denounce you. I knew from the very beginning that you were there. I saw food being carried up there and I saw a new jacket on Mishka [the woman's son]. Putting that together with our prewar relationship, it was easy for me to guess you were there. My brother and I have only friendship and respect for Master Bauer. It is only my brother's wife, she baited me purposely. I

only mentioned your name to hurt *her*, not you." And so, inno-
cently, he had hurt us. We believed him, for we knew him to be
an honest and decent man. Evidently, Mrs. Orsiawski had started
the quarrel to make the neighbors aware of our presence and, in
this manner, to have an excellent excuse to get rid of us.

13

At Pani Blawadowa's

DURING THE DAY, village boys sometimes ran around the hut, pulled at the door, played nearby, and peered inside. Although we managed to avoid being seen, we held our breath when the children were around. It was not a secure hiding place.

With the aid of the widow, Helka, our former protector's cousin, we contacted the current tenant of our manor house. When the Soviets occupied our estate, the house was converted into a school and the teacher, Pani (Mrs.) Blawadowa, lived there. Pani Blawadowa was of the Polish aristocracy. An officer's wife, she was patriotic and good-natured but flighty and careless, sort of a happy-go-lucky person, even in adversity. It was her parents, the Rosas, to whom our estate was rented for the last two years before the War. We visited them, we would see them in the city, and the friendship was warm and proper, even elegant, especially when they entertained us in their aristocratic salon. Out of the formal salon settings, we (the children), and their daughters and son had a great time frolicking in the outdoors. Sadly, with the men of her family in Siberia, only two sisters had survived the cruelty of the harsh forced labor they were put to by the Soviets. There was not a trace of anti-Semitism in her family—and she took us in. We spread out on the floor in our old bedroom and searched for words to express our gratitude.

Mrs. Blawadowa lived in one room of the house and, with peasants helping out, managed on modest means to support herself, her two children, and the family's ancient maidservant, whom she now tended herself—and her cheerfulness always made her frugal table complete. The woman's warmth affected us, our spirits rose, and we allowed ourselves the wild thought that perhaps this safety would last. I recall the day she brought a piece of chicken for each of us. The surprise was so overwhelming that we could hardly speak as we tasted a piece of heaven.

Sometime in May 1943 two young brothers, the Breshers, wandered in from the city, and she let them stay as well. They had escaped the murders in the city and were trying to reach their old neighbors in the next village, Laskowce, where they had grown up. During their few day's stay with us they told of the horrors they had experienced in the city: after the two-day February akcja, the remaining Jews were collected into designated streets, a ghetto in which death, hunger, typhus, and misery were commonplace. The conditions in the crowded dwellings alone were enough to breed a plague, but the Nazis had a diabolical plan to accelerate the spread of typhus. The boys told us that in one of the street round-ups in late December 1942, men, women, and children were brought to the prison where they were tormented and beaten. The Jew-catching on the streets lasted several days, until the prison was full. Then, with a sufficient number of intended victims gathered in one place, they were shipped to Chortków, a neighboring city, where the Gestapo headquarters was located. Escorted by the Ukrainian police, the trip to Chortków was one of punishing misery and suffering.

There, as later reported by survivors of that transport, their reception into the Chortków prison was terrible. First, the Gestapo and the Ukrainian police beat them mercilessly with iron bars, whips, sticks, and rocks. Then, once in their prison cells, they were stripped of their clothes—men, women, and children together—searched for valuables, clubbed, and tormented further. Ribs cracked, heads and faces bleeding and swollen, the prisoners continued to endure beatings, most to a state of unconsciousness—or death. After several days of this brutal suffering, through hunger and thirst, those still alive—and waiting for death to take them—realized that their torturers suddenly became generous. For a couple of days the Jews were given a few grams of bread, small portions of "dishwater" soup, and pails of water from which they were to "drink all you want, you can ask for more." Barely alive, the Jews eagerly drank the water—not realizing that it had been "fortified" with typhus bacteria. Shortly thereafter, they were released, much to their surprise. After such monstrous treatment, to be free! They returned to Buczacz and, of course, spread the typhus. It became an epidemic of disastrous proportions. (The account of the typhus-infected water in Chortków is also described in *Alicia—My Story,* written by my cousin, Alicia Apple-man-Jurman, one of the imprisoned Jews who survived.)

The Bresher boys also told of another akcja and how the survivors of this more recent slaughter were being shipped to other cities: Chortków, Tluste and Kopyczynce, consolidation points to facilitate future annihilation; the Buczacz ghetto was to be liquidated and the city made Judenfrei. The scramble for life was fierce; the young escaped to the forests and others built deeper bunkers, ran to villages, or tried to pass as Christians with false documents. Listening to the Bresher boys recount this and so many other heartbreaking events, it seemed there was no hope for us Jews.

My brothers sat with these two emaciated, exhausted new friends and listened to their account of the unending string of disasters in the city. Rumek had been saying, "If it comes to it, I must kill at least one of the mad dogs—I'll die easier. Oh, a gun, I need a gun!" Now, seething with anger and highly animated, Rumek came to life in his desire for revenge, not even perceiving how impossible such an action would be in view of the hostility toward us by the local people. The adults listened in silence and sadness and wondered how much longer the suffering would go on, our silent questions evaporating into the air.

I recall a midday mealtime when three peasant women came to visit. As our hostess's patience grew thin with the women's long stay, she began to feed her children and got her guests involved in feeding them as well. Then, with a full plate of soup behind her back and walking sideways, she opened the door and "flew" in to us. We were stunned. Sitting by the wall, facing the door as it opened, the peasants saw us—a roomful of hidden Jews—and left shortly thereafter. The conversation among them had become awkward, the children's frolicking was no longer amusing, and the one obvious topic to discuss was taboo.

There was no malice on Mrs. Blawadowa's part; of that we were positive. Yet, we knew she had a flighty nature, and we became concerned for our safety. "No, no, you don't have to leave," she insisted. "To hell with them, they did not notice." But we knew better; we knew the danger such women posed, especially one of them, a garrulous, meddlesome type. So, once again, driven by fear, we left. Where to?

14

Into the Fields

THERE WERE NO FORESTS in this area, so we chose fields of grain stalks. We sat in the wheat fields and changed location whenever peasant voices, especially youngsters, scared us off. We stole into a barn for the first night, moved on, and then came upon a large barn standing isolated in a field on the edge of Mateuszówka, a neighboring village. Half of the barn was filled with hay, and the other half consisted of only a roof supported by poles. We settled on top of the hay, grateful for the roof and feeling some degree of security; at least it was better than the open field. Only an ugly owl staring at us from across the rafters spoiled our temporary "good fortune"—and seeing that black creature was somehow deeply depressing.

Because food was scarce, as always, we contacted two pre-War village elders with whom Father once had a friendly relationship. Pan Wasik, a man respected for his integrity and dignity, had been the Polish sheriff under Polish rule. When we approached him for help, he would not take payment for anything, remembering Father's friendship and generosity. The other, Elder Supczak, was the sheriff under the Soviets and continued as sheriff under the Nazis; he was the head of the village at that time since no one else was qualified for leadership. Supczak committed us to his brother's care and, in this manner, helped us occasionally. We would have turned for help to the brother and his Polish wife anyway, for we had given them some of our valuables for safe-keeping before we left the city. (After the War, the wife returned my family photographs to me.) Thus we arranged to pick up a bundle of food (bread, cooked potatoes, or cooked congealed corn gruel) every week from either Mr. Wasik or Mr. Supczak; our pick-up, however, was more often every other week because of the amount of fear in the air.

After the second week of hiding in the barn, troubling sounds

from the surrounding fields began to abrade our nerves and, by
the third week, we had to leave. Peasants working the land,
greater traffic in the fields, and, above all, youngsters snooping
everywhere spelled too much danger. And then a man, possibly
the owner of the barn, arrived in a wagon carrying tools and
supplies and parked in the open part of the barn. We were petrified with fear and barely breathed or moved until nightfall. Feeling fortunate that we had not been detected, we disappeared into
the darkness of the surrounding grain field. Although the stalks
were high, there was no real security among them, for summer
work brought the peasants out. So we kept changing location,
which was actually worse, for the crushed grain stalks gave away
the fact that *"Zydy tu byly"* ("Jews were here"). I recall hearing
those words when a gang of urchins ran by a few feet away from
us. Whether it was wise or not, we moved around anyway—away
from danger, we thought. Day after day, sitting bent over or flat-
tened on the soil, depending on the height of the stalks, we nibbled on the ripening grain kernels to supplement our diet.

In the course of our erratic wanderings, we came closer and
closer to our old village, to a section called Parcelacja. This land,
parceled out to Poles shortly before the War, was often referred
to as the Polish colony, and Father had made many friends among
those new farmers. We tried for a night's shelter but, instead,
encountered a new blast of hostility. The peasants acted as if they
were crazed and infected with a mad frenzy; they would not even
look at or be near a Jew. They simply slammed doors on us and
chased us. We tried house after house and were shooed away.
One peasant, whom we had considered a friend and who was
known for his mild disposition, was unrecognizable. We stole into
his stable anyway, without asking, and then ran out into the night
when he evicted us in a fury. Unwilling to believe it was the same
man, we attributed his nastiness to the fact that he was ill with
cancer. Had it been the average peasant throwing us out, well,
that was "normal" behavior in those days. But a good, decent
man, a friend—his behavior was a severe blow and it hurt terribly.

We soon heard that a new decree had been issued: the death
penalty for anyone harboring a Jew. No doubt this accounted for
the increased hostility we experienced. What should we do?
Where, where could we hide? It was the end of June, the harvest

was about to begin, and the fields would soon be bare. Perhaps we should head back to the city, an incredible suggestion! Perhaps we could squeeze into some kind of shelter or, even better, go into the forest. The boys were in favor of going into the forest, thinking they might join some escapees who had guns. We decided on the forest.

15

Seit Sich Merachim ("Have Mercy")

WE CHOSE THE FORESTS around Buczacz, but before starting out we wanted to find out what was happening in the city. Bronia and I went to the Malika family, where we were met at the door with "*Bojcie sie Boga* (Fear God). Do not, you cannot, go there. The blood is running in the streets!" After offering us a quick and agitated summary of the horrors in the city, Mrs. Malika handed us a note from a woman in the city and a piece of bread, and then hurried us away with a single word: "Go." The note was from the widow of the man who had been Father's partner in the estate. It read: "*Seit sich merachim, Yiddish Blit giest sich in die Gassen, gefint mir a Behaltnis, ich beit eich, ich beit seit sich merachim.*" ("Have mercy, Jewish blood is running in the streets. Find me a place to hide, I beg you, please, please. I beg you have mercy.") Find her a place? Find *her* a place? we repeated bitterly. Broken, defeated, and despairing, we returned to the grain field.

God! How long, how long, how much longer? How much can the human spirit endure? Despite these thoughts, we tried to sleep and, in the morning, we faced one another still sobbing. The thin slice of bread gave us the heart we needed to do battle with the hopelessness of our situation—and it was, indeed, hopeless and bitter. Mrs. Malika had told us that the hunt for Jews in the city and in the countryside was continuing, that the ghetto in Buczacz had been liquidated, and that any Jew, wherever found, was to be shot either on the spot or in the cemetery. To give the local population an incentive for denouncing the Jews, five pounds of sugar per Jewish head were offered as a reward—whereas harboring Jews was punishable by death. This decree frightened everyone, and rumors of the punishment meted out to protectors of Jews were encouraged. Even if the punishments were never carried out in our region, the rumors spread quickly, and the death threat greatly reduced even the limited assistance initially offered to Jews.

In her hurried report, Mrs. Malika had also mentioned "the second front. America has joined the War!" With that, our spirits leapt! We had been longing, hoping, living, for this very news, confident that our deliverance would be rapid. So close, so close, on the brink of freedom! "America has joined the Allies!" rang in our ears and rallied our hearts. We'll be free in no time, only a few days, a week or two to get through—we have to! God, please! But meanwhile, where shall we crawl so that we might survive?

In our bittersweet emotions the bitterness prevailed. We realized, even as Hitler's empire began to crumble, that the greater his disasters, the fiercer his attempts to annihilate us. The early weeks of the edict against aiding Jews shocked the peasantry and the townspeople into maddening hostility toward us. Our benefactors, although much restrained by the harsher penalties, still had some feeling for us and let us pick up bread along with some sympathy, but our contacts were short and swift. With genuine concern and sadness, Supczak's Polish wife advised us to move away from the place where we were hiding because it was too near to Puszkary—a treacherous village. A band of Ukrainian patriots—so-called Banderowcy—was combing the territory for Jews. Taking her advice, we moved closer to our old hamlet and redoubled our guard for any suspicious sound, fear draining away our diminishing reserves of endurance. Sometimes at night, in pitch-black darkness, we would stretch out our bodies, standing with our arms and hands extended, wishing to reach through to the heavens so that our pleas might be heard and answered.

A Moment of Freedom

I RECALL a July afternoon when the sky darkened and a rainstorm, such as Noah may have known—a downpour of giant drops—opened up on us. Father's delicate health was easily affected by this kind of bad weather, and we always worried about him. As the storm threatened, we covered him with all the rags, coats, and jackets we had, and then the four of us crouched across him to protect him when the rains came. He was covered from head to toe, our bodies forming a kind of tunnel. The rain pelted us intermittently.

Eventually, the heavy rain slackened to a light shower for another hour or so, and then the sun came out. We wrung out our clothes and, with the sun warming us, made light of our earlier drenching. At least we had gotten a bath—the first since we'd left home! Suddenly we realized that during the storm we had experienced a sensation of freedom, a release from the pressure of constant terror. After all, none of Hitler's dogs would come out to hunt Jews in such weather!

With the beautiful sun shining again, however, our tension and anxiety returned.

In an Abandoned Hovel

WE KNEW EVERY HOUSE in the little hamlet near our hiding place, and the boys sometimes ventured, very cautiously, into their vegetable gardens and picked whatever they could. One night they noticed that one cottage was completely dark, its windows blocked with straw. The next night they forced a window open—and we moved in.

The cottage, only a little more than a shack actually, was packed to the ceiling with straw; only a narrow path to the door had been left clear. We climbed up into the cottage's small attic and settled ourselves on the side that did not face the next cottage, which was owned by an unfriendly Ukrainian peasant. We knew that the cottage belonged to Berenko, who had been the foreman of the team of steady farm workers on our estate. He was a sturdy, rough man, who perhaps would not kill a Jew himself but who certainly would not stop the killing of one. We did not know where he lived, and we did not try to find out.

Although we appreciated the God-sent shelter, we knew that the unrelenting hunt for Jews continued and that the cottage alone would not protect us. We needed to create a secret hideout—somewhere to go in an emergency. With a few tools found in the cottage, we dug a trench in the earthen floor of the small hallway and covered it with boards and camouflaged it with straw. We made an opening to the trench in the wall under the oven in the next room; we simply had to enter the opening and slide in. Disposal of the dug-up earth was a problem, of course; we couldn't risk piles of dirt being noticed around the cottage. Thus each night the boys carried out the dirt—pail by pail—and spread it around in the field.

In later weeks we talked about it and realized that the whole project was fragile and useless. If any thugs had actually entered the cottage, we would have been discovered in a minute. What made us do such a useless thing? It had been an effort of desperation driven by the belief that we could survive.

After this effort we just existed, listening for outside sounds, always on guard. If the night was moonlit or held any other threat, we had to skip the bread collection. This meant we had to conserve a portion of the food for a "rainy day." As time went on, we grew to value quiet: our own and the quiet of our surroundings. For example, each morning our dear father would rise early, before dawn, to clear out his lungs so no one would hear his coughing at that early hour. As for our conversations, they were kept to short exchanged whispers so as to make as little noise as possible. Sounds from the outside stressed our nerves and increased our heartbeats; we grew to fear any unusual noise, any human traffic, any voices. Day after day, we sat in that dark, stuffy attic waiting, waiting, waiting, for that longed-for moment of release, all the while our feeling of euphoria about the "second front" and an imminent rescue slowly evaporating. The attic actually grew to feel like a prison to us. Yet we were grateful for that prison; we felt fortunate. But the boys were at their wits' end.

We became infested with lice and, try as we might—constantly combing our hair with a broken comb and rubbing our clothes with wads of straw—we could not rid ourselves of them. The skin on Father's hips began to peel. Hungry, thirsty, hurting, sick, infested with lice, and maddeningly frustrated, we continued to remind ourselves not to sin by complaining, for the fate of the Jews on the outside was even worse. Day after long melancholy day merged into long weeks and months, with constant strangling fear keeping us "active" and on guard. When we made our bread pick-up one week, Mrs. Supczak included an old newspaper that contained a small paragraph about a sort of brawl, or disturbance, and fire in Warsaw. The final line read "All was contained, under control, and tranquility continued."

Mrs. Supczak also told us that something was brewing, something had happened, there was some ferment somewhere, but she didn't know what. That news, even with its vague indication of some activity, raised our hopes and spirits a few degrees. We knew nothing of an Auschwitz or any other death camp; we knew only about the Borki labor camp. The Belzec name was a mystery at the time, and we rejected the rumor that it was a death camp. I only learned after the War that the "disturbance" in Warsaw was the Ghetto Uprising.

At another meeting with Mrs. Supczak, we learned of the fate of the city woman, Mrs. Garben, who had begged us for help in finding a place to hide. She had no choice but to make an arrangement, hesitantly, with her maidservant for the shelter of her son, herself, and Leika, who had somehow joined with her family, in a village some distance from us. Mrs. Garben had originally hesitated in making these arrangements, because of the maid's unpredictable nature. We knew this about the maid; although she could be a good person she was a devil when she was angry. Mrs. Garben's son and Leika went with the maid to prepare a hiding-place in an attic, and the next day the maid was to return and pick up Mrs. Garben. When she returned, however, she was just in time to see the last Jews in Buczacz leave. Grundwaldzka Street was packed with spectators absorbed in the parade of creatures that had once been human beings. The maid joined the crowd to see what everyone was so intently watching: a line of about thirty skeletal Jews, wilted, crazed, shadows of humans, being led up to the cemetery to their deaths. This group of Jews had built themselves a sturdy bunker, those poor souls, deep under the cellar in a solid, massive building, hoping it would be impervious to the Nazi scourge. It wasn't.

That particular fine June day, the Gestapo, with the police and both canine and "human" dogs, besieged the building and flushed out the last Jews with tear gas. Mrs. Garben, however, would not come out. Weeks before, she had said that she would never give herself over to the Nazis. Gestapo soldiers simply tossed a grenade into the bunker—and so Buczacz became Judenfrei.

These sorry reports only intensified our gloom. Between our fear of the outside world and our "prison" life on "bread and water," we fell into still deeper depression. Meager nourishment, constant vigilance for any threat, and heartbeats always at a tense gallop turned our days into one long, unrelenting, unforgiving ordeal. Hoping against hope, we persevered, each of us with thoughts of the past and hopes for the future.

18

Adonai Echod
("The Lord Is One")

I RECALL the time we heard an unusual commotion near our cottage. At first, we heard jumbled voices and shouts—and then we saw groups of Gestapo walking along the road that passed in front of our door. We also heard a youngster running around the cottage, poking at things, banging on the walls and windows, and jiggling the door. Just as we moved the straw away from our lookout window so we could see what was going on, the boy appeared—and we didn't know if he had seen us. To our stricken minds it became evident that the Gestapo men were a raiding party and the boy was leading them. Convinced that a murderous attack would soon begin, we rushed to our covered trench, our little "bunker," and crawled in.

I will never—can never—forget those moments. It is easy to write the bare facts. Eight words: "We feared discovery and went to our bunker." But can mere words convey how we bade farewell to one another, our immense grief and despair, our fear for one another and for ourselves? Can any words impart our devastating heartbreak? The Gestapo was literally at our doorstep—and we felt certain that our death was only moments away. How can I describe our last embraces, our convulsive grasping, our cleaving to one another—our tears, tears, waves of tears. My dear father, my Tatko, was praying quietly: "*Shema Yisroel Adonai Elohainu, Adonai Echod*" ("Hear, O Israel, Lord, our God. The Lord is one"). With precious minutes to live, there was a rush to express love, to say a forgotten something, to live a lifetime in minutes. Grief, love, agony, anger: All poured out in bitter despair, and those memories remain etched indelibly in my heart. "I cannot kill even one of them!" said my brother's eyes, flashing with angry frustration.

We crouched there in our covered trench, barely breathing, fluttering hearts beseeching God, wordless love and heartbreak speaking through a language of tears. Then a faint murmur; "*Fridziu, Danken Gott, du host nisht . . .*" Father was whispering to our mother: "Thank God you have not lived to see this. I lead our children not to the wedding canopy, but to death. God had taken you in time. *Adonai Echod.*" My dearest Bronia, caressing us, stroking us, and consoling Father, started to breathe with difficulty, her breaths coming in short whistles. She labored to inhale and, clutching her chest with one hand while pressing us tightly together with the other, she expelled broken words to help keep our dying hope alive. With Father praying for all of us, we waited, dying before death came.

And then, unexpectedly, they were gone—and we remained undiscovered. We were reprieved, for the moment. There was relief, yes, but no joy, for it meant only that we were condemned to a life of further unrelenting fear.

Reports reached us later—the Gestapo was searching only for partisans that day.

I suspect that Bronia suffered a heart seizure or some sort of cardiac attack there in our bunker, the Gestapo at our door. The years of struggling for survival, the wear and tear of constant fear and deprivation, the February massacre which she had witnessed and so narrowly escaped, plus this experience: all this most certainly had to have taken its toll.

19

Rosh Hashanah—High Holy Days

SEVERAL WEEKS PASSED before we recovered from our brush with death. Slowly, we resumed our miserable daily routine and found ourselves even grateful for that confined life.

The passing weeks brought us to September, and Father calculated, "Next week will be Rosh Hashanah." We then realized that, in the midst of our troubles during the spring, we had forgotten Pesach. To compensate for this omission, in a kind of combined conversation and petition, we prayed, "Lead us out of this bondage, split the Red Sea of blood, lead us, O God, to the promised land." We celebrated the High Holy Days with little bread and much prayer. Fervently we read all the supplicatory passages in the siddur, our prayer book that we had so carefully preserved. Father recited additional holiday prayers from memory, while the boys repeated after him the prayers they had not yet memorized. All was said in whispers, of course. The *Shmoneh esrei, Kaddish, Yizkor,* all of the *Avinu Malkeinu*—"Nullify all evil decrees against us, nullify the designs of those who hate us"— could not have been pressed on the Almighty with more persuasion. When Father intoned the *Kol Nidre* his voice broke, and when we prayed *Shema Koleinu* ("Hear our voice, O Lord"), God could not but know the depth of our need.

We fasted on Yom Kippur. With the morning slice of bread added to our evening portion, we broke the fast and prayed in accordance with tradition: *L'Shana haba'a B'Yerushalayim* ("Next year in Jerusalem"). Celebrating a holy day felt good and lifted our spirits somewhat. The yoke of anxiety, however, was clamped back on very soon.

One night, at the bread pick-up, Mrs. Supczak's brother-in-law, the sheriff, gave us a small bottle of honey for Father. Tatko blessed the honey, took a long swallow, and blessed the man for providing the gift. "May only good fortune be his for life. I feel ten kilos of strength and health coursing through my body!" We watched him and, indeed, it was as if he were a wilted plant whose leaves had come to life with water.

Was it only coincidence that we received the honey while it was still the holiday season? We wishfully decided it was symbolic. In emotional, stirring voices, we cried "Tatko! Tatko! It will be, it must be, a sweet year!" *"Ich gleib, ich gleib—Ani ma'amin"* ("I believe, with perfect faith"), he proclaimed, his voice a vigorous and steady whisper.

20

"They Shot Rasin!" and *"Dus Raiftaleh Broit"*

PERHAPS IT WOULD NOT BE a "sweet" year, but we had found a good shelter in that grim, dusty hovel. We were still captives, of course, but remembering the scourge on the outside helped us to keep from complaining. But sometimes we would voice our rebellious comments and direct them toward heaven. Then we would glance up at the roof that "blocked" our plaintive murmurs from reaching their destination—and return to an appreciation for the safety of that very roof.

The Ukrainian owner of the cottage, our former farm manager, appeared about a week after Yom Kippur. Imagine our fright at hearing the cottage door open and someone entering. The owner was understandably shocked and angry, but also angry with himself for showing his emotions. He liked the *man* Father was, not the *Jew*, and his few words and downcast eyes made the admission and betrayed the conflict in his mind. Here was his former boss, his master, who had treated him with respect and friendship, who had been generous to him, who had been genuinely interested in the well-being of his family. No doubt he remembered how the area peasants had called Father *dobryj pan*, "the good master," and this memory must have bothered him. Yet, it was not the master but the Jew that incited his rage. There was no negotiation, just the rash and harsh Ukrainian command, "Leave my house." Then he ran from the cottage as if from a plague, angry with us and with himself.

We had no choice but to return to the open fields, where many sections had already been harvested. Although the daytime temperatures were still pleasant, the nights were cold and our threadbare coats gave us little protection. Still, we settled wherever cover was available, despondent at finding ourselves without secure shelter once again. We knew that all the fields would soon become flat plains of stubble, depriving us of the little protection they now offered. As we wandered in search of concealment, we eventually reached the village of Mateuszówka, where our two bread suppliers lived. We inspected the open barn carefully to see if we could occupy it again, but it was not suitable; there were too many signs of the farmer's presence. For the time being, the last grain fields would have to shield us.

I recall the quiet afternoon we were lying in a field and heard a gunshot, and then another, from the direction of the village. Our hearts stopped for a moment for we knew intuitively that a Jew had been shot. To us the shots had a terribly peculiar, cruel, and ominous sound. Bronia's face was ashen and she gasped for air. "I know the sound of that shot," she murmured, "the dread in that sound. For two days, for two days I listened." Somehow we felt the heaviness and nearness of death that Bronia felt, and we sat motionless in sorrow, once again facing the brutal reality of our lives.

Late that night, when Bronia, Rumek, and Molus went to the village to get bread from our providers as usual, they found the village still awake and in an uproar. Bronia and the boys were chased and told, hysterically, "They shot Rasin! The Gestapo! The Gestapo! Go away! Go away!" To escape clusters of gossiping peasants, they took different winding paths and somehow became separated. Bronia returned to our spot alone, distraught about the lost children and the situation in the village. In later visits, when the excitement had died down, we were told what had happened.

A Jewish grain merchant named Rasin had been hiding in the home of his Christian girlfriend. Their relationship of many years was a public "secret," and it was understood that that girl would shelter him. The SS and Ukrainian police ambushed her house, dragged Rasin out into the yard, and shot him right there under a tree.

The villagers were quite beside themselves; this was a sensational event. But then the realization dawned on them: nothing, absolutely nothing, was done to the girl or her family. They had sheltered a Jew, yet they were not executed or even punished in any way whatsoever. So the rumors of a death penalty were, indeed, just that, rumors—rumors encouraged to scare and thus prevent anyone from attempting to rescue a Jew.

Later that night, Bronia returned from the Supczak home alone. My brothers had reached the Wasik home, but they were not taken in. Instead, they were thrown a piece of bread, the small end-piece of a loaf, and were then chased away. Running in the wrong direction, they wandered about most of the night trying to find us, but actually strayed even farther. When the sun rose and daylight spelled danger, they simply had to hide in the grain field. Needless to say, Father, Bronia, and I spent that night and the next day in a state of constant anxiety.

Early the next evening the boys found us and immediately gave Father that paltry piece of bread. As they told their story, we sat and listened in silence. All through the night of fear and the following day of hiding, my brothers had not eaten a crumb of that bread—at an age when, it is said, a teenager could eat a horse. Rather, they saved that small treasure for their father. Although we never talked about it, we understood that every little piece of support, whether it be bread or hope, would help keep Father alive. Bronia and I struggled not to cry when Father asked, "Why didn't you eat *dus raiftaleh broit* (the heel of the loaf)? You should have. You needed it . . . a whole day." The crack in his voice betrayed his deep feelings.

We eventually moved nearer to the Polish colony because we had no food. There, we dared to raid the vegetable patches, pulling carrots and beets. There were potatoes, but uncooked they were indigestible. The grain kernels supplemented the vegetables and, later, the bread pick-ups resumed.

Then it was October, and the nights grew cold and the days varied; it was fall. With the rains coming and the land bare, where, *where*, could we crawl so as to be invisible yet sheltered from the elements? Shivering and huddling together one day, we considered all possibilities. "Why don't we try Mrs. Blawadowa at the manor house again?" one of us suggested. With winter coming, we had to at least try, even though we were bothered by the fact that Mrs. Blawadowa's visitors had seen us and that the manor house might now be unsafe. But we had no other option.

After knocking gently at the doors and windows, we found, much to our surprise, that the house was unoccupied. Experts by now, we crawled in through a window and took possession.

THE "FINAL SOLUTION"

Let me speak before Thee, O Lord!
The world lies in darkness,
and the dwellers therein are without light,
for Thy law is burnt!

from *Tevel Sumah Bachoshech*

Back in Our Manor House

ONLY TWO ROOMS in the house were empty; the rest of the house was packed with straw. In one corner of the dining room we made a bed with some of the straw and fell onto it gratefully. The windows were still shaded with our own old *rolety,* cloth shades, and we hoped it would add to our security. As a routine set in, we even performed a few housekeeping chores. Once in a while we prepared a small fire using a few pieces of straw—so as not to light up the room at night or make smoke that would betray us—and cooked soup with a potato, a little flour, and some muddy water from the unused well.

Across from our house the only cottage left was occupied by a mean Ukrainian peasant family, which meant that we had to be especially careful. The whole estate, except for our house and that cottage, which had been the milkman's home, had been demolished; the estate management and workers' housing, farm buildings, orchard, and gardens had been leveled. The grounds had become a thoroughfare for foot traffic and farm wagons.

Although we were anxious and fearful, we were grateful for the shelter this building provided. Constantly watchful for our own safety, we also watched for any signs of ultimate liberation. But time passed: first December 1943, then January 1944. When an occasional airplane flew over—a new and astonishing occurrence—our hopes soared, but at the same time, the report of a murdered Jew would destroy that hope. We got the news that Dr. Chalfen from Buczacz was shot in Dobropole, and then we heard of Jews being murdered as they straggled along the roads. Such news, along with our bodily misery and constant tension and anxiety, wore us out. How long? How long? Our fervent and imploring murmurs joined Father's daily recitation of *Tehillim* ("Psalms").

I recall how we welcomed the snow of that winter. When a

small snowstorm would grow into an angry blizzard, raging furiously and piling up snowdrifts as high as the house, we relaxed. Normally dreaded, the storm was beautiful to us, and a soothing respite from fear. Our emotional shackles would fall off, inner tensions would loosen, and we would relax for the duration of the storm. It was a welcome pause when we could catch our collective mental breath, knowing that even the most determined Jew-hunter would not oblige Hitler in such weather. There was, at the same time of course, a depressing realization: the knowledge that there were Jews stranded in that same snow, unsheltered, unprotected, dying.

We continued to hope and to hold on to the belief that we would survive. Mrs. Supczak, our bread supplier, continued to provide us with bits of news. "Yes," she said one time, "the front line is nearing. Hitler is retreating." But we had heard that before and had rejoiced at the news of a "second front"—and yet there were no discernible results that improved our conditions. Thus our spirits didn't rise with such news. I recall when another airplane flew over, surprising us once more, giving us a glimmer of hope and prompting some bold speculations—then it was back to the old misery.

Meanwhile, the Jew hunt went on, our distress redoubled, and everything worsened. Our Tatko was suffering, for both his hips were raw from lying on hard floorboards and his delicate lungs needed serious medical attention which, of course, we could not provide. Rumek developed a nervous tic, pressing his lips together and giving a sort of dry spit. Then I got a bladder infection, and passing urine became a knife-slashing torment. Bronia prepared hot compresses for me, and the excruciating pain eventually passed. All of us simply had to make do with old-fashioned home remedies.

I recall one morning when Rumek, sipping his muddy water, stared intently into his cup. "What do you see there in that cup?" I asked him. "Quiet," he responded. "I am studying the germs; their dance amuses me." And then, as he gave two of his nervous little spits, I noticed his unusually round, full face. "You know, Rumek, with all the starving and all the suffering through these ordeals, you look pretty good," I told him. Then, almost as an afterthought, I added, "It must be last week's extra potato. I was stuffed."

"But you do, too, and you also, Molus," said Rumek, this comment directed at his brother, who had just awakened. Then Bronia got up, and we noticed that she, too, was fairly plump-faced. As we mockingly lauded our diet, knowing our faces were simply swollen due to our poor diet, Father arose—we suddenly broke off in mid-sentence, shot looks at one another, and immediately resumed babbling nonsense to mask our shock. The right side of Father's face was swollen; in fact, his cheek was hanging. We felt wretched, realizing that the life of our beloved father was ebbing away; anguish, misery, and pain were draining his vitality.

As February arrived we noted that the frequency of airplanes flying overhead increased: from once, then twice a week and then to every day—and our spirits dared to rise. Naturally, when we received reports that "Hitler is retreating," we were invigorated. Then, when the airplanes began to appear twice a day and sometimes more often than that, it seemed to us that the Nazi defeat was imminent—and we became cautiously ecstatic. Something must be happening, for surely the planes are smashing the wicked bastards. But we prayed silently, "God, please protect us now more than ever. It's so close. Free us from this agony." As the encouraging news reports increased and we heard that the Soviets had broken through the German lines and that the front was nearing us, Father calculated that we would be liberated by the holiday of Purim.

Oh how we hoped! "Any day now. Any day now! Please God! *Please.*" We would survive. We would force food into Tatko's empty stomach, help him regain his old strength, and oh, we would be free! Free at last. Crazed by the sound of each new airplane roaring overhead, ever wilder in their plans for the future, the boys sat on "pins and needles." Fidgeted, and bustled about, impatient to enjoy the sunshine in the open air of freedom. They had "tasted" it already; we all had, and for the moment, we could not let the tragic horrors of recent yesterdays spoil that special feeling of an imminent, longed-for walk into the sun. The reality was, however, that we were still very much alone in a jungle of hostility, even if we were within reach of freedom's waters.

Day after day, beneath the roar of air traffic, my young brothers built "castles in the air," and the sound of happy plans for a new future was heart-warming. They had different plans every day. Yes, they would get their education, a profession, but that would come later. First, food! *Food!* They created visions of juicy meats, butter and cream dripping from fluffy breads, and luscious fruits. We could practically taste those dreams as we swallowed saliva. On another day, apparently after consuming all that "food," my brothers would make plans to study law, medicine, theater, engineering, writing, and more. Enjoying our eager anticipation, we were able to forget about our hunger, our cold, our vexing aches and sores—but we were never able to forget the persistent danger that surrounded us.

After the organized akcjas in the cities, surviving Jews had to be pointed out and denounced to the Nazis. The Germans could not identify a Jew on the street, for generally a modern Jew was hardly distinguishable from a Christian. Their distinctive dress, of course, identified many Orthodox Jews, but an emaciated, wretched appearance eventually gave away all Jews. Indeed, faced by the Nazi apparatus—the SS, the Gestapo, and the Ukrainian police—it was difficult to evade doom in the cities.

In contrast to the cities, in the countryside the presence of the Nazi machinery was not very visible. The Ukrainian police were stationed in only the larger villages of the district, and they had to summon the Gestapo or SS to carry out any killing of Jews. It was not that the Ukrainian police could not "legally" do the killing themselves, but reporting the capture of Jews gave them a favorable loyalty record. Once in a while the Germans would join with the police to track partisans, guerrilla fighters, and on those occasions, they often trapped fugitive Jews as well.

The Ukrainian gangs of thugs, the Banderowcy, made the work of the Gestapo and the SS easier by scouring the land, pulling Jews from their pathetic hiding places, and killing them at will. If only the Ukrainian majority had left us alone—or even if they had not cared if we lived or died—half of the Jews in our area would have survived. If they had remained neutral to our fate rather than collaborating with the Nazis, so many more of us would have lived. They certainly realized much gain in what they did. Those Banderowcy gangs had the opportunity to rob their victims at the scene of the killings, as they did with my own family. There was no "legal" justification for them to report hidden Jews to Nazis. They simply wanted to see us die.

22

Horror

OUR FUTURE ENDED March 8, 1944, when the Banderowcy surrounded the house and stormed the door. By the same door
through which the sun had awakened us to life each day, over the
same threshold on which we had sat as children, the assassins
struck. They entered our home and murdered my family. Two
weeks later, on March 23, the Soviet forces broke through. They
were two weeks too late.

When the murderers stormed the door of our house that night,
fear paralyzed and strangled us. At first, we were petrified stumps
of horror, rigid and numb. Then, our instinct to survive overrid-
ing our fear, we sprang into action in a desperate attempt to escape. As Father gasped *Shema Yisroel*, we supported his fragile
body and ran for the straw-packed rooms on the other side of the
house, hoping to find a secure place to hide. We had gone barely
a step when we saw that it was too late. As the door was yielding
to our attackers, we turned back. The hunter was pouncing on
his prey and was about to seize us.

With a new surge of energy driven by terror, we ran for the
windows in the back room. "Jump!" Bronia commanded. In a
wild frenzy, my brothers and I scrambled through the window,
Bronia lifting and pushing us. But where? *Where* should we run?
How could we hide? We were like trapped, crazed animals, cringing in terror. Behind us we could hear Hitler's accomplices charg-
ing through the door and crashing into the house, dogs barking,
owls hooting and screeching in a wild rage. There was havoc in
the air and panic in our hearts. *Where? Where?* our hearts
screamed. Which way to run? I clasped my heart to keep it from
jumping out through my mouth, all the while my brain whirled
with insane horror. I was numb, stunned, terrified. *"Run!"* Father
implored, half off the windowsill. "They are inside! *Run!*" commanded Bronia. *"Run!"* my brother Molus gasped in a fierce and
desperate whisper.

And we ran—in wild, blind, maddened terror. I saw nothing as the world around me merged into a nightmarish blur. I simply ran—insanely, headlong, into hell. A shot rang out, the dogs howled, the owls on the roof . . . Oh, I will never forget those owls and their shrieking, piercing cries, screaming with urgency as if urging us to flee the carnage to come. Those owls—together with the dogs barking, the hysteria, and the shots—became a shrieking tempest in my brain. My heart seemed to fall out of my body and the fear that pushed it went for my jugular—and I continued to run blindly. There was no wall, no crevice, not even a scraggly tree, to use as a place to hide. The milkman's lonely shanty a few yards away, filled with Ukrainian hostility, was in full sight of the killers and therefore useless. All around, flat as a table, was a vast plain of glittering white snow and an angry full moon glaring down on a white night crackling with fire. Driven by raw fear, I ran, ran. Then a blow on my head hurled me to the ground and, for a short second, I grasped for air. But the impact of the blow turned the world dark and I fell, sprawled unconscious on the snow.

When I awakened, I was giddy and disoriented but remained inert; my eyes would not focus. As I tried to regain some mental power, I sensed that someone was standing over me. I opened my eyes just enough to see black boots—and I quickly closed them again and remained motionless while the murderer stood over me. Suddenly, possibly thinking me dead or at least sufficiently disabled, he left to help in the capture of my escaping family. I did not know where we had been running—and I still do not know when or how we became separated. Once the thug left me, I got to my feet, dazed and disoriented, and crawling at first, I tried again. Actually, my instinct ran, not my legs; I could not. The snow was knee-high, my feet were bare. I stumbled, I crawled, I ran—in spirit, away, away from a nightmare.

My pace slackened as the questions pounded my brain. To whom should I run? Where should I go? I cried. I talked to my-self, carrying the magnitude of my loss like a band around my heart. "Tatko, tatko drogi, Tatusiu, Broniu, dearest, children. They must be killing you now! God, please save them, help us. Mamusiu in heaven, dearest soul, beg for us, please, please, God!"

I continued to run and crawl, my mind a swamp of desperate

delirium. To whom should I turn? Who would take me in? Where could I hide? Then, moments later, despair overwhelmed me. Why should I run? What for? My loved ones are slaughtered, there is horror all around. It is an evil world and I can expect only more suffering. Besides, there is no way to escape.

I didn't want to live—but I didn't want to die. I pressed on, away from the manor house, fervently mouthing a plea to God and the world for deliverance. But in answer there was only God's mystical silence and the world's indifference or hostility.

I was so frightened, so forlorn, that dreadful night on the open, snow-covered plain. There was a full moon, and I knew that running figures would be clearly visible to any pursuers. I had to decide if I should go to the neighboring village, but I knew that our peasant benefactors would turn me away on such a moonlit night. We had always selected dark nights and out-of-the-way places to meet our peasants for the bread pick-ups.

My bare feet were frozen stumps and I was practically naked, wearing only a thin, threadbare cotton dress. I shivered with cold, sobbed, and talked to myself. "Why? Where am I running? I don't want to live. Yes I do. Yes. No. Please, God, do not forsake me. Lead me. . . ." I stumbled on, crawled on, walked on, without direction—just away from the evil.

Suddenly, I saw moving shapes across the field. I felt as though I had frozen into a pillar of ice. My mind screamed, "They have found me! They are coming toward me!" I think my soul flew away. I reeled and felt myself disintegrating. Gripped by fear, I burrowed into the snow. From deep within me, with uncontrollable sobbing, I implored the Almighty with incoherent supplications: "God please, I don't want to die. I don't want to see them, to see death gloat over me, not again. I don't want to see the horror again."

I curled myself still deeper into the snow, wrapped my arms around my head, and pressed my eyes deep into my knees. I didn't want to see the coming ugliness, yet I could hear death's footsteps crunching in the snow, coming toward me, coming closer. I mumbled every prayer I had ever learned and remembered. Only God knew what I meant.

As the crunch on the snow neared, I pleaded for a miracle with new urgency—and each new wave of sobbing ripped my heart to pieces. And then the footsteps stopped. Death had arrived—and I dissolved in agony.

"Co sie stalo? Co sie tam dzieje?" A Polish voice asking, "What happened? What happened there?"

Had I really heard a soft, concerned voice in my world of howling fury and chaos? Had I actually heard a voice of decency in the midst of savagery? I couldn't believe it. I stopped sobbing and remained still, lying in the snow, curled up with my knees to my chest. After a few moments, realizing that the non-threatening voices were not an immediate danger, I slowly straightened my body and looked up to see three men, obviously upset, reaching down toward me. These were Polish youths who were guarding their colony from attacks by Ukrainian marauders. They knew my Father, recognized me, and half carried me to their colony. *"Mój Boze, mój Boze"* ("My God, my God") exhaled from the very depths of my soul, and that was all the young men could understand from my confused babble: "My God, my God."

23

I See, I Hear, I Walk with Them

MY RESCUERS TOOK ME to the Sawirski household, where I sat
like a zombie between the bed and the oven. I had felt the touch
of death, yet my skeletal, limp body and tortured soul had survived—but my father, my sister, and my two brothers had been
murdered that night. In my mind, I was with my dear family on
their march to death. I could see the despair on their faces, and I
knew their terror as they were led away from the village into the
fields and knew they were to be shot. I could see it all.

With their usual swagger, the Banderowcy squad boasted about
their crime, and details of the murder reached me later. The children had half-carried our dear barefoot Tatko. He was wearing
only his ragged shirt, and only the embraces of his children kept
him warm. Using the few pieces of gold he had saved to buy
food and shelter, Father pleaded for the lives of his family, but the
taunting answer was, "We'll have both, your lives and the gold."

While Father was immersed in prayer, trying to stave off the
ultimate agony, Bronia became violently emotional. Appealing
to whatever spark of humanity might rest within the monsters
surrounding her and her family, she must have spoken with her
heart on her lips, as only despair can speak. But her pleas could
not melt the iron inflexibility of the killers, and she was cut short.
The drama made for good boasting by the murderers and was
enjoyed by their listeners, who thought nothing of the killing of
Jews. As for me, with the mental picture indelibly imprinted on
my memory, I struggled to keep sane. I still do.

My dear father, dearest Tatko, a most benevolent, gentle soul.
How we had hovered over him. How we had sheltered him
through the years. How we had huddled around him to keep him
warm with our own body heat. Day after day, we let the hope of
a second front nourish him, convincing him that he and his family
would live to see liberation. Why, God, did so honest and giving

a human as my father have to undergo the indignity of an ugly death? Why so much suffering, so much pain? Are the good and the just fated merely to endure while evil triumphs?

I remember as a child, I saw Father walk into the house from the farm with a very dejected expression. I heard him talking to Mother, saying, "I couldn't embarrass him. I saw Pawło stealing grain. He was scooping it out through the granary cellar window. But I could not embarrass him. If he steals, he must need it. He has a brood of children." The thief was a peasant farmer who worked on our farm whenever extra help was needed, but it never occurred to Father that this man was simply greedy. In fact, Father thought all humankind was good. He believed others would do as he did and could never "embarrass" a wrongdoer. He would let himself be hurt, but he could hurt no one. He was the definition of a good man.

I thought of my beloved sister, Bronia, unsurpassed in her de- votion to her family. I thought of Rumek and Molus, those young saplings, my baby brothers, still innocent of life. I thought of Monio, "the scholar," my own twin brother, the first murder victim. They were all cut down mercilessly. To this day, I am absolutely certain that had the boys—or at least Rumek—had a gun, a Nazi thug would have fallen with them. Rumek, increas- ingly frustrated, had repeatedly cried, "If only I could get a gun! If cornered, I want—I must—first kill a Nazi!"

Hitler zealously went about completing his "final solution," and the number of his victims mounted rapidly. Of my family of seven, six were no longer a "problem" for him. Monio, eldest of the boys, had fallen in the first Nazi atrocity in our city. Mother, although she died before the War, had bitterly tasted the poison of cruel, vicious anti-Semitism. And now Father, Bronia, Rumek, and Molus were gone.

24

The Funeral

FIFTEEN DAYS AFTER THE murder of my family, the Soviet forces liberated the territories of Eastern Poland, and the Russians marched in. At long last, I was free—it was really true. Should I step out and scream . . . for joy? for grief? Yes, there they were, the Russian soldiers. From the cottage window I could see, in the misty distance, a column of soldiers making its way past a neighboring village.

I was drawn into the peasant family's excitement as they pointed and shouted, "See? Look! Look! Russians! Russian soldiers!" Laughing and smiling, I repeated, "Yes, the Russians are here," while unspoken, the words "too late" hammered at my temples. In that moment I suddenly realized that I was, indeed, liberated; I was free. I could breathe the fresh air of freedom, see the sun, and call out, "I am Jewish!" And then a spasm of indescribable pain pressed in on my heart and only a cheerless whimper escaped me. Two weeks earlier my family was murdered, and I alone survived. My family did not live to taste this moment, suffering so much only to be massacred in the last moments before liberation. How we had envisioned our happy return to the city! What dreams, what plans, what hopes! We would get on a horse and wagon and, all the way to the city, we would shout and sing in defiance, "We are Jews! We have survived!"

Then we found the bodies, four of Hitler's victims: Father, Bronia, Rumek, and Molus. Everything inside me heaved up at the gruesome sight. Janek, the fifteen-year-old Polish youth, came with me to help bury them. He tried to steady me. I could not utter a word; only a kind of hiccup, an inhuman sound, escaped me. In my agony I could only think, Why, God, why? The body of my dearest Tatko, so kind, so honest, goodness personified, lay intertwined with the boys. A yard away were Bronia's remains.

To be separated from the others meant she must have fought like a tigress—but with only her intellect for a weapon, it must have been like reciting poetry to a hyena. If only I could scream!

I followed Janek's instructions and dug the grave. I dug, I hit, I slashed at the earth, carving out a grave deep and wide enough for my dear people. Janek then helped me carry the bodies and lay them gently to rest. Although he was young, Janek had the maturity and intelligence of compassionate understanding. "We cannot just bury them without some prayers," he said—and with that, something somewhere within me snapped. God, what have you done? "Tatko! Tatusiu! Look who is saying Kaddish for you! You had three sturdy, healthy, dutiful, loving sons to say Kaddish for you. They each put on the *thephillin* daily for morning prayers before school. They found time for the *Mincha-Ma'arev* as well, between the schools, and you beamed with pride! Now," my soul cried, "look who is saying Kaddish—a *Shaygetz,* a Christian!" Anger and pain choked me, so much so that whatever prayer Janek murmured, I did not hear. He may have even included some *Yezus Christus* words for all I know. Thankfully, it was all incoherent to me; all I heard and felt was that he, the Shaygetz, and not my father's sons, was praying. My nails dug deep into the spade handle, pressing it deep into the earth, and my heart sank with it.

When Janek finished his litany, he began to cover the bodies, and the stone automaton that I had become followed his instructions as though in a trance. My heart clung to the grave as it received my beloved family. I spoke not a word. I said nothing to God either; in the riot of emotion in my mind and heart, I had lost sight of God. Finally, I spoke to Janek and thanked him for his help, his kindness, his thoughtfulness. He surely meant well by the prayer, and I appreciated his sensitivity.

Time passed in questioning and arguing with the God I was not yet ready to see. Then it came to me; just as the sky is still there whether I look at it or not, so is God—my father's God, the God of my loved ones. God is one with them, and they are mine. God is mine! God did not kill my loved ones; human beings did, human beings who did not obey their consciences, human beings deceived by evil, human beings no longer governed by conscience. And it is conscience that elevates humankind to humanity. We need conscience, love, ethics, and morality to secure peace for our children. The commandments of conscience will guide us away from evil—and God will help us. We must listen.

THE LAST 100 DAYS IN HITLER'S HELL

> My heart doth writhe within me;
>   and the terrors of death are fallen upon me.
> Fear and trembling come upon me,
>   and horror hath overwhelmed me.
>
> Psalm 55:4–5

Return Home

I RETURNED to the city within a few days after the burial. Bundled up in an old tunic, kerchief, and dried-out pair of shoes donated by the peasant family, I stepped out into the road not really believing that I could actually show myself and walk freely in the open. One of the girls from the family went with me, and we plodded through the March snow to Buczacz, fourteen kilometers away. I recall how the sun was shining that day, its rays caressing me as I gulped the air of freedom. But just as the March winds cut the sun's warmth, the clouds of grief churning in my heart dimmed the sunny joy of liberation.

I found our home in the city empty except for two smashed and doorless wardrobe closets and a trunk filled with trash. The windows and doors were broken and the inside walls were caved in. Both our home and our family had been destroyed.

In the center of the city Jews milled about, greeting one another amid tears and laughter—mostly tears. I met one of my former classmates, some acquaintances, and other Jews I knew who had lived in Buczacz, but I did not know them personally. It was estimated that about eight hundred Jews had survived in our town, and the Christian population seemed unpleasantly surprised at such a large number. A Ukrainian woman named Mazulka said to me, "We did not know so many Jews still remained," and her face betrayed her deep regret. "Next time they won't," she added sharply.

We all began to pick up the pieces of our lives and tried to regain some degree of normality. I found Leika, the neighbor's daughter who had been with my family in hiding from time to time, and Berko, the boy with whom she had been hiding; they had survived! I joined them and together we went to Leika's former house across the street from mine, where the current occupants gave us a room. Our new landlady and her family, Ukrainians, protested that they "loved the Jews" and tried to oblige us in every way. Somehow we managed to feed ourselves. I don't know where the food came from, although I do remember a plate of soup from the landlady, bread that I had brought with me, and a bundle of cornmeal from the village. With our immediate needs of shelter and food met, we were drawn by and into the current of life.

Leika and Berko went to town every day to mingle with the surviving Jews. They milled about, consulting one another, seeking advice on starting life anew—but mostly they gathered to console one another. People talked of their past horror and revealed their hiding places, even to the Christians. I stayed home most of the time, nursing a bad throat and the sores on my feet—the skin had frozen as I ran barefoot through the snow to escape my family's killers. With time, the skin thawed and then wrinkled, wasted, and became tender. My stiff old shoes had made the sores worse. I rested on the bed and, with homemade remedies, both my throat and my feet began to heal.

It was the end of March 1944, and new clouds began gathering as rumors circulated, rumors that proved to be true: The Germans had counter-attacked and were pressing back to the city! Fear and tension returned, everyone believed that there would be only a few days of skirmishes, a week at most, and the Germans then would be driven back. All we Jews had to do was hide for a while and we would survive. But in two or three days, as the German advance continued, the search for new hiding places became frenzied because people had revealed the locations of their "bunkers"; there *was* nowhere to hide! Before we had even enough time to catch our breath, the nightmare was upon us once again.

Leika and Berko ran back and forth between our house and town, bearing bulletins of alternating bad and good news. One day they went to the center of town, but did not return.

After the War, one of the few survivors told me about that night. Those desperate Jews who had absolutely no place to hide had assembled at the headquarters of the Soviet military, begging for advice, direction, and help to escape. But all the soldiers, officers and enlisted men alike, were drunk—and kept on drinking themselves into stupidity. Hostile, drunk, and often anti-Semitic, they jeered at the pathetic flock and chased the Jews away, ignoring their entreaties for help. They would not, or could not, tell the Jews how far the Germans were from the city. Then, when enemy shots were heard from behind the school only a few blocks away, the Jews began to run. The whole miserable crowd of about three hundred raced between trucks, horses, tanks, and equipment of war. They were chased, overrun, crushed, and many were killed. In that pandemonium, Leika and Berko were carried along into flight and oblivion.

As the night grew longer with no sign of Leika or Berko, I realized that disaster had come upon me as well. In the morning, in conference with the landlady's family, all of whom now were a little less "loving," the conclusion was, "Do what you like, what you can, but find somewhere else to hide." I examined some cellars and pantries in abandoned houses, but nothing could serve to conceal me.

The next day, with German soldiers already in the streets, I changed into my peasant clothes and headed toward the same village that I had left only two weeks earlier. About half way there, I reached a large lake near Medwedowce and was stopped by a Soviet soldier standing on guard. "Who are you and where are you going?" he asked. I explained and begged him to let me pass. Although he seemed to sense my urgency and was sympathetic, he could not help. "This is the front line," he explained. "If I let you through, you will be considered a spy and shot, there is no doubt about it." My God, what am I to do? Where am I to hide now? I thought again of my family, of dear Bronia who always took care of everything. Without a lifeline, I felt forlorn and desperate, left to rescue myself. I turned and dragged myself back to the city.

When I arrived in Buczacz late in the afternoon, I went to the home of our landlady's brother, the Swistels. Although Mr. Swistel was not a mean man, he was a drunk and easily aroused to anti-Semitic actions. His wife was a dull and sorry creature, and all but one of his sons were Nazi sympathizers. The three Swistel brothers, a predatory lot, were not at home; they were busy hunting Jews. The one exception was a boy who was crippled, and he was my protector. That teenager, good-natured, likable, and friendly, whether at his shoe-repair bench or hopping around on his crutch, had been our playmate before the War. In a way, he offset the bad instincts of his family.

Although the family let me in and gave me something to eat, they didn't say much—but I stayed. The next evening the house filled with company—their young friends and a few German soldiers—and I put on my best Christian face so as not to spoil the jolly evening. The boys all knew who I was, but one look from my handicapped protector spoke the order—and kept me safe.

German soldiers were everywhere, however, and in the following days, my safety became more and more uncertain. I moved to the attic and then to an empty room in another house, but the soldiers swarmed in and out of all the buildings. Mr. Swistel advised, "You should go, you must go," saying this while soldiers were actually in the yard, passing under our window. That evening, Mrs. Swistel brought me a bundle containing about half a kilo of dried, toasted bread; she did not need to tell me what I should do.

26

In the Attic

I REMEMBER that it was almost dawn as I ran breathlessly across the street into our former home and climbed up to the attic. I thought that I would squeeze myself into some corner or a depression between the roof and rafters, and cover my hiding place with attic rubbish.

I think God must have taken me by the hand and led me to that hiding place, for I had never seen it before. But there it was—and it was for me. I saw it in the first gray light of dawn: a blind wall—a double wall with a narrow space in which to hide. Gasping with disbelief and emotion, I crawled in and shut myself off from the outside. That was the end of March or the first days of April 1944. Nearly four months later, on July 22, 1944, I emerged from there more dead than alive.

My hiding place was a kind of crawl space over our verandah. Evidently someone had built the cubicle as a hiding place after we had left the house. The outside wall had been doubled, hiding a foot or so of space, leaving one board opening from the inside. For the moment, I felt relieved and thankful. About a week later, however, thirty or forty German soldiers moved into the house!

I recall that morning clearly. "My God, I'm lost," I gasped. "Please, God, save me." Frightened though I was, I kept telling myself that I was safe, that nobody knew where I was. Besides, in a few days, a week or so, it would all be over; the War would end. I made my jacket and kerchief into a pillow, put the bread at my feet, and . . . and what? Not yet hungry, I sat there and probably dozed off, but then the street below seemed to wake up. I looked out through a tiny hole at the edge of the roof and saw civilians and German soldiers rushing about. I untied my bundle and had a slice of bread for breakfast. There were ten, maybe fifteen pieces of bread of various sizes. At one piece a day, I reasoned, I would have enough to last me until the War ended.

By this time, Buczacz and its vicinity had become the battle-field. Cannons roared from the front lines and the din of shooting resounded in the distance. The German soldiers slept in the house, left in the morning, and came back at sundown. Only one remained on the premises during the day, apparently in bed, for I could hear him coughing day and night.

I spent my time sitting, lying down, sitting up again, and lying down again. To stretch, I would sit up; to rest my upper body, I would lie down with my knees bent. Confined in that little compartment, I had nothing with me or around me to keep myself occupied. I kept counting my slices of bread and thinking, "It won't last long. The War can't last much longer."

But as the days passed, my optimism began to fade. I started dividing each remaining slice of bread into halves, then into quarters, thinking I had a supply for twenty days, then forty days. The War would no doubt be over by then. No, not forty days, God forbid. Surely it would end much sooner. Actually, I cheated; I ate the crumbs as I divided the bread. I had originally allowed myself half a slice of bread each day, then only a quarter slice. Then, as time went on, I allowed myself smaller and smaller pieces—and the crumbs. I was constantly hungry and thirsty.

With nothing but fear and discomfort to occupy my thoughts, I constantly relived the assault and murder of my family. I could remember everything in vivid detail: the storming of the door, the paralyzing fright, those ghastly, screeching owls, the flight into the night, the dogs howling, those black boots standing over me. I relived every moment of that night of horror, the image of the bodies of my beloved family strewn in the field, and their burial. It had been only a few weeks, and the horror was still fresh. I could not escape it.

I tried not to sleep for fear of betraying myself with a snore, a breath, a move, but I must have slept at times. I remember one night being awakened by the sound of whistling just below me on the verandah. A soldier stood in the doorway gently whistling and smoking a cigarette—I could hear him exhale. I barely breathed and felt lucky that he did not detect me.

I gradually grew feverish and thirsty—not hungry, but so very thirsty. I pleaded with God: "Please send some rain!" If it rained I could catch a drop through the hole in the roof. And all the time, the film projector in my head continued to spin, circle, and churn the scenes of that night of horror; it would not stop. While soldiers went up and down the streets, in and out of all the houses looking for loot, while people were passing every which way, I sat counting and re-counting my bread—as if playing a game—and through all that the horror scenes kept replaying themselves in my head. My mind saw only the murder scenes. The images flashed by, from beginning to end, full cycle, again and again. "Please," I begged God, "I don't want to see it. Please, I beg you, God. Make it stop!"

Three or four weeks passed, and I could not bear the torture any longer; I could not go on, my head was on fire. I pressed my fists into my eyes to squeeze out the sights, pulled at my hair to remove the images from my mind, and silently screamed. I was so thirsty, so very thirsty; my lips crackled against the friction of my dry tongue. I felt crippled. Plagued and drained, my whole being seemed to dissolve into agony, and I slid down onto the floor, resigned and inert. As I waited for the end, *water* was the only thought I could express—*water*. I was dying. It was my fourth week without a drop of water.

Then came the crisis. I remember awaking that early dawn, silently screaming from a macabre dream involving the Gestapo. Suddenly I felt light—the fire and riot were gone from my skull, and images of the murder ceased. I lay there flat, limp, and exhausted—and extremely thirsty. My mouth was dry and parched and my tongue and throat felt swollen; I could hardly swallow. I felt needles stinging my eyes.

Suddenly I heard a pounding, a rhythmic thumping. Although I remained motionless, I could identify neither the direction of the sound nor its source. When several attempts at spying yielded no results, I gave up. Then, after the pounding stopped, I raised my hand for some reason, and there it was again—the thumping of my own heart. I was so weak that the effort to move my hand had set my heart to pounding. I repeated the gesture to test this out. It was then that I realized I was dying, not of hunger but of thirst; thirst was strangling me. With hammers banging at my temples and pins stabbing at my eyes, I rebuked myself, "Do something! You will wither away and die if you don't do something."

Within a day, an opportunity for me to do something presented itself. As usual, only the coughing soldier remained in his bed that morning after the others had left for the day, so I braced myself and dared to act. Weak as I was, I forced myself to climb down from the attic and go to the kitchen. I knew the arrangement of the rooms, of course—this had been my home. I also knew that the noise would not disturb the bedridden soldier, for looters regularly entered houses and made all kinds of noise. The most precious thing I saw as I stepped into the kitchen was a pail of beautiful water. W-A-T-E-R! My heart pounded and, for a second, I shook with indecision. Soldiers were swarming back and forth, passing by the windows and doors, going in and out of houses; I knew I was in great danger. But I saw *water*. I believe that I would have charged at that water even if there had been a guard nearby threatening me with a gun. Water was all I saw— and I flew to it, fell upon it, and drank my fill before I stopped to draw a breath.

I was determined to take the water up to my attic hiding place, so I started the struggle of pushing and dragging the pail toward my destination. It was terribly hard to climb over stools, boxes, and other debris and not spill it, and I eventually became sorry that I had even begun the project: Why did I do this? I felt lost! I continued to fight with the pail, however, because I *had* to have that water!

I finally reached the attic, where I had planned to push the pail into my small enclosure and be done with it, but I realized that the pail would not fit through the one-board opening. When bending the pail did not work, I shivered with tension and searched the attic for a smaller container. Finding only a few dirty bottles, I poured the precious liquid into them, spilling some on the attic floor, and placed the empty pail in a corner. The freshly spilt water posed a terrible danger, though; it could betray me, but I had no choice. I quickly crept back into my minuscule shelter.

Not five minutes later a German head appeared at the opening to the attic. He was not looking for me, only robbing the house and looking into the attic for loot. Had he come up and noticed the wet floor, I would have been shot, no doubt about it. Most robbers did come up and search the attic. In fact, a week later a soldier crawled into my verandah area and took a good look around. He could not see me, but I could see him through a crevice between the boards. Our eyes seemed to meet, and I froze. I stopped breathing for what seemed an eternity. He examined the place on all sides and went away—and I breathed again. A week after that, the soldiers left the house completely.

Counting my pieces of bread became my occupation, and a calendar of sorts—each piece of bread consumed meant another day had gone by. Four more pieces for this week, seven for next week—and each week I split the pieces into smaller and smaller portions. By mid-May I had water, but I was very hungry.

My verandah was only about three feet from the road, so I was able to see activity and catch bits of conversations. Every morning, for example, I saw Russian prisoners of war, a whole squadron of terribly bedraggled wretches, marched somewhere and returned in the evening. All the while, people walked up and down the streets and soldiers ran about plundering whatever they could from the empty Jewish homes. I recall one morning seeing a crowd of people, their necks craned looking up the street. "What is it? What is going on there?" I heard a latecomer ask one of the spectators. "Oh, nothing special. They found more Jews. There they are now on the hill on the way to death. It's a long line today." At first, this scene was repeated every other day but grew to be a daily event. I also heard that the city was to be evacuated.

One day in early June I saw a pre-War neighbor, a woman I knew I could trust, pass my verandah. "It's Tunia," I called out to her. "Please bring me some bread." This angelic woman was about thirty years old, but she looked seventy; she was terribly ill with asthma. Because she was a Polish woman, her husband's Ukrainian family barely tolerated her. I remembered how my mother, sister, and I often nursed her and helped her when she was really in need. Needless to say, she was startled by my call but, toward evening, she brought me half a round loaf of black bread and confirmed the news about the evacuation.

Indeed, a few days later, I noticed crowds of people gathering in the streets and rushing about with bundles and parcels. In particular, I noticed two frightened, dejected faces: the children of Dr. Silbershlag, a teenaged girl and a boy of about nine. The distress in the young girl's face was obvious. She was a curly-haired redhead—and that gave away her identity for, in Poland, a redhead was likely to be Jewish. Although the girl had a heavy green shawl wrapped around her head, it didn't "protect" her. I learned later that both she and her brother died.

As the evacuation got under way, only essential manpower—mechanics, electricians, and the like—remained in the city with their families. In the following weeks, traffic in the street lessened, but there were still enough people to gather in small clusters to watch the executions on the hill, which happened with depressing regularity.

One day I saw a woman—presumably the mother of an engineer or someone who had been allowed to remain in the city—in the house next to mine. She looked, I thought, motherly enough to feed a beggar. I did not know the woman, but my hunger was so great at this point that I took a stupid chance. When she happened to wander into the small flowerless patch in front of my house, I called out to her and asked her to bring me some food. She was understandably startled and hurried off to her own house where, five minutes later she walked out, carrying a tray of food, and proceeded to eat "in front of me" with an exaggerated relish. I was grateful, though; after all, she could have denounced me.

While the killings on the hill continued, German soldiers went about robbing buildings and tearing down porches, roofs, doors, carrying off everything that was portable. I feared for my verandah's safety and, consequently, my own. And I was so very hungry. It was the second half of June and I was counting my daily rations over and over, cringing with hunger, cowering at the killings on the hill, fearing the wild soldiers, and sagging with despair. This hell, this *przekleta woina*, this damned War—was it never going to end?

The nights gradually grew quiet and the streets deserted. On one still, pitch-black night, an idea struck me: Why shouldn't I go down to find food? I recalled seeing grain, corn, and beans in the attic of the house across the road. Slowly, cautiously, I climbed down from the attic, groped my way across the street and into the attic, and found a treasure of grain and beans. Back in my niche, I gorged myself on stale and moldy grain, rubbing off the mold by grinding each kernel between a cloth. Although the beans really were inedible in their raw condition, I chewed them anyway to extract any possible nutritional value. Adding my dirty water to the meal, I had a veritable picnic.

It was July when the bombs began falling, and the remaining civilians—the work force and their families—were upset. I could hear the women crying and see them running back and forth, wringing their hands, calling, "They hit here! They hit there!" Unashamedly, I enjoyed their distress. Although a bomb fell on a nearby fence, it didn't bother me; I remained calm. In fact, I was elated. Something was going on and I interpreted it as beneficial to me. It was the German and native rats prowling and hunting after me that I feared.

As I nibbled on my grain, the July days passed slowly. That little amount of food helped me combat my anxiety; they were literally grains of hope.

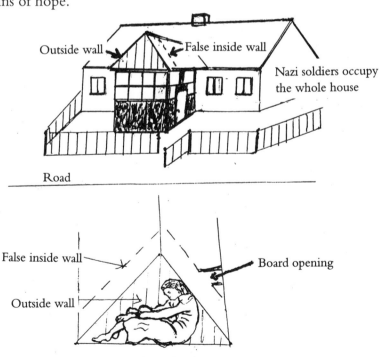

27

Liberation

I REMEMBER the day I saw a tank, then another, and then *katyushas* (rocket tanks), trucks, and long rows of military machinery. For several days long lines of katyushas appeared on the road and passed in front of my house. I didn't know what it meant and was only afraid that the long-shelled tubes of the katyushas in the narrow street would bump and shatter my verandah. The din—the roar of the moving weaponry—lasted three days, and then everything stopped. Life in town stopped, and a ghostly silence followed.

The next night was eerie, black, dead. I considered going down for food, but the thought had hardly occurred to me when a piercing, prolonged whistle—once, twice, and a third time— ripped through the air. It was late—well past midnight—and I scolded myself for wanting to venture out. I realized later that it was a Soviet patrol.

The next day the Soviets arrived in force, but I didn't see them because they marched into town along the main highway. Sometime later, I heard voices beneath me, on the verandah—speaking in Russian! *"You see, this is what they left us,"* someone said, kicking at something.

I was stunned and bewildered; I just did not believe it. Although I could see only one side of the street from my lookout, it was clear that the Soviets were sending teams—a Russian officer and a civilian—to do house-to-house surveys. Well . . . I drew a long breath, but I still sat there unable to believe it. Did I really see a Russian, hear people speaking in Russian? Could this be an illusion? Could I really step out? I did not trust my eyes; after all, it was only a glimpse.

Not sure, my heart pounding in anticipation, I waited—the rest of that day and all the next. The day after that I saw a Jewish girl, Matylda, walking along the street and scrutinizing every house. Well, then . . . we *were* liberated.

Dazed by that realization, I slowly crawled out of my hiding place and climbed down to the rooms below, to our home—my home. I have returned! I was here! I was alive! And then the deafening silence of the emptiness made my heart plunge and my spirit screamed: *I have returned . . . alone, alone, one of seven.* Hitler's macabre machinery had emptied this house, and the full extent of that tragedy stared me in the face with a new force. Everything converged on me, everything in the room spoke to me—every corner, every nook, every mark, echoed with the past. From the very depths of my soul a cry escaped up to heaven, but my body slid to the floor in a heap, half senseless under a mountain of pain. All the grief, all the suffering of the hellish years, all the sorrow, burst my heart and the accumulated pain came pouring, spewing out. Like smoke billowing from a burning house, cloud upon cloud, so did the memories stampede one upon the other. It was a seizure of uncontrollable sobbing—no more constricted, silent crying—and the tears flowing so freely seemed to carry off some of the grievous weight.

In that paroxysm of heartbreak, I recalled the images of my lost loved ones—and I populated the room with those images. I saw all of them and my heart longed to reach out to them. I spoke incoherently to my dearest Tatko, to Mamusiu—imploring, wishing to have them with me, wanting them all—sobbing. I called out to Bronia and my brothers. I saw them all and this time, I did not want the visions to go away.

I don't know how long I sat there, my whole being convulsed with sobs. Exhaustion gradually lulled me into a calm stupor, and my sobbing subsided. I could sleep at home now, I thought, but another look around—there was my bed, there was that memory; voices spoke to me—and I could not bear it. I flew back to the attic and, completely spent, slept there one more night.

The following day I went out of that house for the last time. As I shuffled along the fence that bordered the street, I saw a neighbor, an old bachelor, standing in his doorway across the street. When he became aware of something moving on this deserted and desolate street, he was obviously startled. As if to confirm that what he saw was real, he moved forward and visibly exerted himself to approach me. Drawing nearer, he crossed himself with his only arm and mumbled some prayer in which I could hear him pronouncing the name of his God. His expression told me that he wondered if he was seeing a ghost or a human being.

The man and his mother, a woman in her eighties, along with their goat, were the first to return to my street. He was a good-natured person, bent on following his brother into the priesthood, but the First World War had upset his plans; he lost an arm and his parents were blinded. His father, a Ukrainian brute, was dead, but his mother was alive, a dear woman. These two kind people took me in and listened to my weak, sluggish whisper of a voice tell my story.

With the first meals, I kept half-fainting, overcome by attacks of nausea. The woman would cook everything with goat's milk, which is very fat and, to a starved stomach that had been inactive for more than three months, the fatty milk was a disaster. "Eat, eat," she would urge me, and I certainly was eager, but with every bite I became dizzy and my stomach heaved with nausea. Desperately craving something sour to counter the nausea and revive me, I ate the red currants I found in the garden near the river. Fruit, of course, was the worst thing for my unsettled system. Eventually, when I began to tolerate the food, my body swelled abnormally, and for nearly a year, I was too weak to hold my body upright. With time, however, I slowly recovered physically.

Of the eight hundred survivors of the first liberation in March, only fifty-five native Buczaczer Jews, including some who later returned from Russia, remained alive. Leika returned without her friend; he had been drafted into the Soviet army and, after only one letter—from a hospital in Riga—we never heard from him again. Eventually, Leika and I moved in with two other girls, Sheindel and Ida Gassner, in the same old room, across from my former home. These girls had jumped from the same cattle train to Belzec as my cousin Alicia had.

My home! My violated, dismantled home—with the windows ripped out and the remaining holes staring like empty eye sockets, each speaking to me in a dear voice of the past. Facing it every day, the wounds of war still fresh, I stood at my window thinking about the sadness and the siege of evil I had survived.

I remember one day, shortly after the War, seeing a man walking out of the common backyard shared by our house and that of our former landlady. Across his shoulder the man carried a huge rolled-up rug that displayed a Greek design. I almost fainted because I recognized the rug. My hands reflexively reached out to it, and I screamed without voice, "It's mine! It's my rug! It's our rug!" It was! It was our beautiful salon rug that had been saved from our country house, Mother's wedding present from her parents. The luxurious rug had a large medallion patterned in the center on a field of geometric designs in shimmering colors of green, sapphire, and golden brown—with a Greek design around the border. It was not the value of the rug that broke my heart; it was the bit of home that it represented to me. A part of my loved ones were in the very fibers of that rug. They had lived with it, played on it, rolled around on it. If only I could touch it, hold it, caress it, I would feel the nearness and touch of my dear family.

The burly tree-trunk of a man carrying the rug had a nasty disposition known to all, and it was prudent that I not step in his way. After all, how could I have convinced him that the rug belonged to my family, to me? I stood there and watched him disappear, my eyes following the Greek border until it was only a memory—and then I had a good cry. They were gone! My family was really, irretrievably gone! I could not touch them, hold them. I could not have them back ever again.

When the High Holy Days arrived, our small community of Jewish survivors straggled apprehensively into a makeshift, improvised House of God. When the reader, my father's friend, Mr. Horowitz, tremulously intoned the sacred verses—"Hear, O Israel"—those of us gathered could not help letting our memories overcome us. As we listened to those words our tears flowed. There, on the platform between the men, next to the reader, I could imagine my Tatko with his three sons, resplendent with the subtle grace of the moment. Instead, the tiny cluster of men embodied profound sadness. Huddled together as though in one family, all of us, formerly rich or poor, educated or not, religious or secular, old and young, were united in grief. We were all orphans in need of a guardian to guide us, a guardian we could trust. How was it that we still remembered to observe and worship the

Supreme Being after so much ugliness? Did we come to settle our grievance with God and, reconciled, regain our equilibrium? Or did we search for the Almighty Protector of old and, in this manner, hope to regain some measure of what was before?

Like beggars searching for shelter in winter, we longed for the warmth of tradition. Tradition called to us and, deeply ingrained, our faith sustained and held us together. We came, then, to confirm our faith in God. Above all, we must have wished to reaffirm and feel God's divinity. We said Kaddish, but not in accordance with the traditional liturgy. Rather, our voices erupting in sobs sounded more like a chaotic shattering of vessels. But we continued. At the conclusion of our prayers, we wished one another *"B'Shana HaBa'a B'Yerushlayim"* ("Next year in Jerusalem").

There was nothing left in Buczacz—or anywhere else in Poland—to hold us, nothing but pain. Under the leadership of Mr. Horowitz—Grandfather—we put up a *metzaiveh*, a monument, for the thousands of our loved ones who were gone. There, at a special memorial gathering in the Jewish cemetery, our hearts said good-bye to those we had lost, and the following year, we left—some for the Jerusalem of Israel, some for the Jerusalem beyond the Atlantic: America; some for other places. Buczacz was no longer part of our world. It was no longer our shtetl.

We learned not to cry, but we also learned not to forget. We cannot forget. We have six million reasons to remember.

EPILOGUE

This chest of memories remained locked for nearly half a century. I carried it with me every day and have felt its weight deep in my heart—but I never allowed myself to raise its lid. I remembered everything, but I felt that to recall how it happened and to mentally review the scenes of the tragedy would destroy my ability to maintain a normal life. In my last months in Hitler's hell, concealed in the attic, I could not tear the images of ultimate despair from my mind, or the visions of the murder of my loved ones from my sight.

After the War, that pain had to be healed, but had I allowed myself to open the lid of that chest, I would have been caught and broken on the spokes of that wheel of terrible memories. I would not have been able to function. It was not possible to carry the burden of the past while living in the present. The past would bear down and crush the present—and we could not allow that. We, the survivors, had to live to spite Hitler's plan to annihilate us, to be living witnesses to his crimes. But first we had to recover.

Now, so many years later, although the hurt has not diminished, a protective, gossamer membrane of time has slowly grown over the pain and, carefully, the wound may be touched. Now the suffering of our people must be told loudly, for the world must know of the evil that human beings have inflicted on human beings, and my generation of living witnesses will soon be gone. Perhaps by exposing this evil we can prevent its repetition and humankind can again lay claim to being civilized.

By exposing my grief to the light of day, by raising it at last from the depths of my soul, I have calmed the aching memories of horror and catastrophe. Once again, I can remember the earlier, happy years; I can see my dear home and remember the laughter, the air of love we breathed, our private jokes, the code words we used, special holidays and vacations, the delights and pains of childhood, and the love of our beautiful mother and golden-hearted father. I see the mass of flaming crimson roses in our garden, and all of us children, intoxicated by the fragrance, picking every morning's freshly opened crop for preserves. I see the giant raspberries and hear the squeal of laughter and piercing scream of a bee-stung brother at the apiary—for beekeeping was Father's favorite hobby and a source of frolic at honey-harvesting time. I see the festive Pesach table, with Tatko propped up in his chair and drinking his wine in the obligatory reclining position. I see the glowing candles in their huge and elegant sterling silver candlesticks, and Mother in front of them radiating a serene holiday spirit. I remember Shavuos, when the dining room was a garden of greenery, the walls and furniture were decorated with green sprigs, and the floor was a carpet of green leaves—and we, the children, shuffling and swishing around on it, much to the annoyance of the adults.

I remember, too, a severe storm one spring, when the rain had not yet fallen; the wind was warm but fierce, sweeping away everything loose. When we looked out the window, Mother exclaimed, "What in the world is he doing?" My little brother, Molus, then four or five years old, was on his way from the stables to the house, bent over and carrying a huge stone under each arm. "What is that for, Molus?" Mother asked as my brother breathlessly tumbled into the house. "You know what, Mommy? In another moment the wind would have carried me away. I made myself heavier with the rocks." I can still hear our explosion of loving laughter.

I also recall the day we were all in the orchard and the boys decided to make a fire from a few sticks of wood and roast corn. They went into the vegetable garden in a fenced-off section of the orchard and hunted for the best ears of young corn. I remained on the swing in the playground, merrily pumping high into the heavens and fancying pageantry scenes in the floating clouds overhead. Suddenly I saw a dark cloud—a swarm of bees buzzing wildly from tree to tree, trailing from the direction of Father's colony of beehives. We children knew, from growing up with bees, what this meant and what a precious event this was for Father: A new queen bee and her brood were searching for a new home. This is a momentous occasion for a beekeeper, like the birth of a baby. Only a skilled beekeeper can draw the swarm out of their eventual nesting place and into a hive. Because Father and Mother were away for the day, I alerted the boys and, in great alarm, we ran to Bronia, who immediately sent Monio for Father's beekeeping assistant. Meanwhile, Bronia and the rest of us followed the swarm through the fields and watched them floating in the air very erratically, buzzing angrily.

We followed them through the fields until they came to a neighboring village and finally settled on a tree near a barn. When the curious farmer emerged and asked, "What do you want?" Bronia explained the situation. "Well, these are my bees," the farmer insisted curtly, his expression clearly indicating his wish for us to leave. "But we followed these bees from our home. These are my bees," Bronia anxiously responded. But the farmer was adamant. "It is my swarm, my bees," he repeated endlessly with no further evidence to support his argument. As a crowd of peasants gathered to observe the scene, we entered into an obvious deadlock. Suddenly the cottage door opened and an old man with a long white beard, carrying a cane, came out. He considered the situation, approached us, and said to the farmer, "What is happening here, Son?" With a straight face the farmer gave his laconic reply: "She wants the bees. They are mine." The older man then turned to Bronia and said, "Let me hear what you have to say, young Miss." As Bronia then explained the situation, with every detail of our pursuit of the bees, her voice broke with emotion while we children clung to her, whimpering. The old man, both hands resting on his cane, looked down at the ground, pursed his lips, and stood motionless. There was silence. All eyes focused on the statue-like sage.

After a while, as if awakened from meditation, the older man pronounced: "Truth has a different ring to it. Son, get in the house. Miss, get your bees." *Truth has a different ring to it.* I will never forget those words.

Joyfully, I ran to meet my brother and the beekeeping assistant. They had been told the direction of our pursuit and were coming toward us with equipment on a cart. We had saved a new kingdom with a young queen and had returned home triumphant—and Father was elated. At every year's honey-harvesting time, our "heroism" was praised once again—and each year another small detail was recalled and retold, and retold again.

Now, when I recall these golden moments and others like them, the tears flow inwardly, silently bathing my heart with their sweetness and soothing the bitterness of my loss.

In all these years, however, there has been one unceasing and unanswerable question: Did my family know that I had escaped? Did they walk to their deaths sighing with relief or moaning with grief for me? As they traveled that too short, yet so long, march toward extinction, did they think that I was already dead?

No, my dearest ones, I escaped—and now I am telling the world to heed my cry and my sorrow, and to understand the lessons of our agony.

And I remember. Forever, I will remember.

A year after liberation, I left Buczacz with a group of Jews and headed for Western Poland and then further into an unknown world. As we boarded freight trains with our meager possessions, my own luggage contained some linen, silverware, a kilim, my brother's watch, one dress, my father's Persian lamb hat, and the remnant of a bolt of dress fabric. All these things were reluctantly returned to me by neighbors after I heatedly insisted they do so. My suitcase was stolen from me, however, as I traveled through Western Poland.

On the train, my friends and I made ourselves comfortable on the straw in one corner of a wagon car. As we shared the food we had prepared for the journey, we speculated about and planned our futures. My traveling companions were my friend Leika and the two Gassner women with whom I lived after the War, under the Soviet regime. They were all seamstresses and worked at home, and I helped them occasionally as I recuperated. Then, after several months, I got a job as an office clerk, earning meager wages. Some villagers had remembered me and helped me with little bundles of provisions.

At the other end of the wagon car, a group of young men celebrated their departure rather raucously with a bottle of wine, joking and glancing in our direction. At one stop, when I had to step outside the wagon and could not avoid passing the celebrating youths, I averted my face because I did not want to grace them with so much as a glance. "See that girl?" I heard one of the men say. "She'll be my wife."

Well—I did become that young man's wife! There was no falling "head over heels" in love, but I came to recognize the speaker's integrity, sincerity, good heart, and straightforward personality. With time, our attraction grew into mutual love and devotion—a love and devotion that lasted over fifty years. Even when he was gravely ill, that man's first and foremost concern continued to be my well-being. Julie died on August 31, 1997.

It was only natural that the groups traveling together on the trains would grow close. Our trips were long, with many unscheduled stops ranging from fifteen minutes to a full day. During those long layovers, people would free themselves from the oppressive atmosphere of the train to find fresh air and relaxation in the surrounding fields. Some of us searched for water so we could wash and renew our drinking water supplies; others tried to prepare meals. Overall, a friendly relationship developed among us.

On one of those many stops, Jechiel, my future husband—although I didn't know it at the time, of course—was cooking a soup. He owned a toothbrush, a razor, boots, and a supply of concentrated soup. Where he got the pot and spoon I do not know, but he intoxicated everyone with the aroma of his soup. Suddenly a Russian official in uniform appeared and demanded that all the men follow him to a warehouse across the tracks to load or unload goods. Because we never knew how long our stops would be—minutes or hours—some men, concerned about getting the work finished in time to get back before the train departed, got ready to do the work. Not so with Jechiel; he simply continued to stir his soup without even a glance at the activity around him. "It is an order, you must come," the officer repeated, but the soup continued to receive Jechiel's full attention. "Give me your passport!" demanded the officer, so Jechiel handed him a paper, all the while crouching over the fire. Pretending he was reading the document, the Russian turned the paper every which way, and then stated, "If you are not coming, you'll never see this document again." Some people watching the scene became alarmed and whispered to Jechiel in Yiddish, "Go, go. You'll lose the papers." But Jechiel did not move—and the officer left with the document and the rest of the drafted men.

Still stirring his soup, Jechiel suddenly burst out with laughter. He had given the Russian an ancient, useless piece of paper with Polish writing on it. After about an hour, the train did, in fact, leave, and those who had gone with the officer missed it. Their friends took responsibility for the men's belongings, hoping they would meet up together soon. Back in our compartment, Jechiel graciously shared his soup with our group, and a friendly relationship developed among us. I was polite to Jechiel, and he was most attentive to my needs. As he told me his remarkable life history, I realized this was a man of integrity, deserving my respect.

As a teenage orphan, Jechiel had moved to Lwów, where he got a job, earned a fair income, and lived quite happily; he even sent part of his wages to his brother in Buczacz.

Jechiel was in Lwów when the Nazis marched in—and life changed drastically. In the first days of the occupation, the Ukrainians were given a free hand and, with exceeding glee, proceeded to murder and rob Jews wherever and whenever they could. When Jechiel, a strong, steely man, spoke of that period, he could not describe the atrocities without his eyes filling with tears. In the second week under the Nazis, he witnessed the hanging of the city's ten rabbis; for days the bodies were left hanging from the lampposts in public display, each wrapped in his own *talit*, his prayer shawl.

One day, Jechiel recognized two men marching in a unit of prisoners from the Janowska camp, a particularly brutal camp; the men, Selig Heiss and Shayeh Furman, were from Buczacz and were already skeletal. From that day on, Jechiel would risk his life to discreetly hand each of them sandwiches as they marched by. Heiss survived, and after the War, when we met at a Landsmanshaft Society gathering, his wife kissed and hugged my "Jechielik" (an endearment) and repeated the story of my husband's heroism at every meeting.

With each day the situation of the Jews deteriorated. After one of the akcjas, Jechiel stole into the ghetto in search of friends. "I shall never forget the scene," he said. "It's still before my eyes." At the entrance to the ghetto sat an old, skeletal Jew who called out to Jechiel, "Young man, young man, come here. Look. Take a good look at the bodies and remember them. Run, run away.

Save yourself. You are young! Run and tell the world what they did to us. Take revenge! *Nem nekoomeh, nem nekoomeh!*"

Then, similar to what the rest of us had experienced, conditions worsened and life became a living hell. When Jechiel approached a friend, a Ukrainian, for false identity papers, he was provided an identification card—and Jechiel Katz became Julian Kozlowski. I shall always remember Jechiel's comment: "There is good and evil in people. Never blame *all* people for evil deeds. My friend was a true friend, a most decent human, and a Ukrainian." And so Jechiel moved about freely on those Christian papers. But then came the day when someone apparently recognized him—and betrayed him.

Jechiel was alone in his room when a Ukrainian policeman walked in. "Papers!" he demanded. And then, after a quick glance at the paper, he said, "You are not Kozlowski! You are a Jew," and he grabbed Jechiel by the throat. Jechiel knew he was lost if he was taken to the Gestapo. In order to live he had to fight—he had no choice. A life-and-death struggle ensued. The wrestling left the policeman badly wounded and "Kozlowski" ran for his life. While he hid in cellars, attics, and sewers for a week, the "lawman" died and an alarm went out for the killer of the "brave servant of the Reich." Jechiel eventually smuggled himself out of the city—nothing short of a miracle.

He set out through fields and forests toward Russia, walking at night, sleeping during the day. For food, he would glean a leftover beet or some corn from the fields and, when hunger pangs demanded, he took a chance and raided a peasant's pantry. In the Ukraine, still under German control, he managed to get a job— still as Kozlowski—repairing and renovating military equipment. With the job came a precious commodity: a food card. He worked with a sizable group of men and, with one look at the way a fellow handled a tool, Jechiel could spot another "hidden" Jew masquerading as a Christian. Jechiel recalled an incident in a secluded area where he calmly spoke a few Yiddish words to another man, who paled visibly and froze on the spot. "Don't worry, me too," Jechiel answered, trying to calm the man with the knowledge that he was not alone. That man, Nusiek Genefeld, was a doctor with a degree from a French university. Jechiel took him under his wing and protected him throughout the rest of their difficulties. Later, in deepest Siberia, when the camp management assigned the doctor to scrub latrines, Jechiel intervened and the man became the head doctor in the camp.

As the German army pressed eastward, the Soviets had to retreat deeper into their land; so did some of the population. Workshops were abandoned or dismantled, and indispensable machinery was shipped further east. "Julian" and his friends, Jews passing as Christians, left their work and fled through the fields and farms, trying to reach Kiev. The skies were raining bombs and military battles raged—they were in the midst of the front lines. They sought shelter in peasants' stables, cellars, and field shacks. Whenever there was a lull in the fighting, they moved on.

In the Ukraine, with the doctor and four other "hidden" Jews, Jechiel finally crossed the front somewhere near Poltawa. They were immediately imprisoned by the Russians as spies and faced the death penalty. After some quick talking, however, they convinced the military authorities that they were not spies but escapees from Hitler. Miraculously, the officials believed them and sent them on to Siberia, where camp conditions were abominable: starvation, sickness, and squalor. Because Jechiel was a metal worker, he set up a shop and made small ornamental knickknacks and utensils that he used to bribe the authorities and, as a result, camp conditions improved. He "made a living," however, by playing chess with the brass—winning a game meant a slice of bread. He fed himself and his friends with the sacks of bread he won.

Then one day, through his friend the doctor, Jechiel discovered a young boy named Lonek from Lwów in the infirmary, in a section reserved for the dying—where "patients" were not cared for medically, just fed watery soup to ease their end. Finding the boy skeletal and close to death, Jechiel suddenly realized that he had a need for a helper in his shop. Jechiel took the young man out of the infirmary and said to him, "You just sit and feed the stove to keep the fire going, and I'll feed you." Jechiel made sure Lonek ate constantly, hoping to rekindle vigor and life in the young but near dead body. Eventually, the young man recovered completely. After the War, I met Lonek and he confirmed Jechiel's entire story. I have a picture of him, inscribed with: "To dear

Julian, who substituted for Father, teacher, and was my guardian, for eternal remembrance." Jechiel had become Julian by then.

And so I grew more acquainted with this man, became interested in getting to know him better, and was soon won over by his decency and natural intelligence. We became friends and kept regular company.

When we arrived at Katowice, our group—of which Julian had become the leader—smuggled itself across the border, climbed the Tatry Mountains, which seemed to reach the sky, and came to Czechoslovakia. There we were promptly arrested and taken to a police station where we were treated badly. Harassing remarks, harsh questioning, and a generally coarse attitude toward us betrayed a biting anti-Semitism.

Eventually, through the intervention of and a bribe from a member of the Jewish Committee, we were released. We fled into a nearby forest, slept there for the night, although it was quite frightening, and then headed toward the German border. From there, German peasants working in the fields guided us to a train station, where the group decided to split up. Julian, Leika, and I left for Stuttgart; the others went to Fährenwald. Through all this, Leika's fierce guardianship of me had been unwavering; I guessed she felt an obligation to care for me as my family did for her during the War.

Once we reached a Displaced Persons camp in Stuttgart, we lived there for a year. I considered returning to school, but I gave up the idea because I simply was not psychologically ready to sit in a class with German students and professors. Socializing with other survivors, exchanging our histories, gathering in the camp's dining room, searching for possible surviving family members, making occasional trips to other camps: these activities constituted our recuperating period. We also waited for affidavits that would allow us to emigrate to the United States, or "Certificates" to enter Palestine, which was still ruled by the British. Although we spent our time attending lectures, meetings, and courses, or venturing into town for shopping or to see a show, all this was just to occupy the time while we waited to emigrate and settle down in a new life.

Julian—"Julie" to me—was my boyfriend by then, but I continued to waver about taking the final step. I liked him very much; I had become quite attached to him and felt secure in his protective attention to me. In other words, I began to love him. But something bothered me. He spoke Ukrainian well, but his Polish was only fair. Most Jews from our region spoke Ukrainian; only the assimilated and those conservative Jews who circulated in a modern environment spoke Polish. We spoke Polish at home. I rather wished Julian spoke Yiddish, which I did not speak but understood. In other words, I have to admit that his poor schooling bothered me. He told me that after World War I the schools were more like battlegrounds between anti-Semitic Christian teens and Jewish boys than centers of learning. I was glad to hear that as a young adult he attended classes and studied Moishe Leib Perelz, Bialik (in Hebrew), Chekov, and others, as well as world history and poetry in Hebrew. Years later, in tranquil times, Julian continued to recite Hebrew poems to me.

One day, while we were strolling in the camp, we discovered a woman sunning herself in front of her building—and I recognized her as a person from Buczacz. Mrs. Hirschorn was an elderly woman, a grandmother, who had survived all alone. Julie, Leika, and I attended to her needs, and she became like a grandmother to us. We bathed her, brought her food from the camp's dining room, kept her room straightened for her, and helped her in many ways. It was good to have a grandmother.

Because Mrs. Hirschorn had known both Julian's and my families, I spoke freely with her about my confused feelings. With a grandmotherly caress of my head, she said, "*Naarale, tiyer kind!*" "Silly, dear child! He is a good man, a decent man. I knew his angelic mother, his honest, pious father. They were poor but a very respectful and respected family. I saw Jechiel grow up—orphaned, poor, hardworking from an early age, and with inborn, inherited integrity. He handled life well. After his mother passed away, leaving small children, the orphans were cared for by family friends—esteemed sages in the community—were given a Hebrew education, and were properly prepared for their bar mitzvahs. "He is a nice young man and comes from a nice upright home," she insisted, "and that's very important. You have to see his intelligence and his gentle, yet strong character." In my mind it seemed to me as if I had been talking to my parents; I must have sensed their nod of approval.

We became engaged. The diamond chips in my engagement ring, although tiny, sparkled with great promise. And what fun Julie had "buying" it for me! Two Germans, the husband of my seamstress and a friend of his, were playing a fierce game of chess—and a single move was about to put one of the men in a checkmate position. Julie happened by near the end of the game, surveyed the "battlefield," and offered, "I bet I can save you." The potential loser said, "Not possible. If you do, you can have this diamond ring." "It's a bet," Julie countered—and he "won" the ring.

In the fall of 1946, after frequent throat infections, it became imperative that I have my tonsils removed. Everything was arranged. Julie secured the best surgeon, using butter, coffee, honey, and other delicacies as payment—and all went well. Then, after eight days, when I was ready to be released from the hospital, my cheek suddenly swelled and I developed a high fever. Although the doctors and nurses were totally baffled and helpless, the chief surgeon, on his weekly rounds, only had to touch my gums to discover the cause: a molar had broken off and the root, deeply imbedded in the swollen gum, had become infected. A year earlier, the tooth had been pulled by a German dentist who had broken it and left the root, all the while assuring me that there would be no problem. And there hadn't been—until now. The surgeon was furious, and I had never heard such ferocious scolding of mature, degreed doctors and nurses for not identifying a cause. My roommates and those attending me did not expect me to survive. Julie was hysterical and, when not importuning the staff, was at my side day and night. Although Leika tried to help, she had her own matters to attend to; she was to be married and was preparing to leave for Palestine.

A dental surgeon was called in, and another surgery was performed. Evidently, it was no easy extraction; it seems the surgeon could not grasp the root from the swollen tissue surrounding it. During my recovery, the doctor would often greet me with, *"Was macht die dicke Backe?"* ("How are you, Thick Cheek?") During my week of recovery I rested, browsed magazines and newspapers, and listened to the stories of my visitors.

There were four other young women in my room, all survivors of the War, and they had their visitors, too. I recall the day I was half dozing and half observing the husband of the woman in the bed next to me. The man's appearance put me in a sort of day-dreaming state; he was tall and middle-aged, and had a high fore-head, a prominent nose, and a weather-beaten face. His height and wind-burned face are actually what intrigued me. "My God!" I realized with a start, "he looks so much like my father! He could be his brother, cousin, something." My yearning for this to be true was so strong that I began imagining all kinds of possible connections, but I kept my wishful thinking to myself. After all, I did not want to interrupt him and his wife. I could not help overhearing them speak, however, and at one point I heard him talking about a conversation he had with someone, saying that this person repeated what a third party had said: ". . . but Pan Bauer. . . ."

Well I practically jumped out of bed. "Sir," I interrupted, "who are you? My name is Bauer, too!" My trembling was so pro-nounced that I could barely speak. The man was as surprised as I was and began asking questions in a chaotic jumble. He had, in-deed, known my father quite well, but he was not a relative—and he kissed me to calm my nerves. "In a way," he said, "there is a relationship. I knew your father since both of our occupations were in the sphere of agriculture. We counseled each other many times." He was an administrator of an estate of absentee owners in Mateuszówka, the village next to ours. As we exchanged our histories, my disappointment was somewhat eased. Years later, we were to meet again in Canada.

Finally, we received our affidavit for the United States of America and had to begin making preparations for the voyage. I recovered in time to sail to America. We arrived in Bremen and were promptly informed of a coal strike in the United States. As a re-sult, all immigrants were detained in a camp for three months and, finally, in January 1947, we boarded a military ship.

Aboard ship, we were pleasantly treated to an exquisite din-ner—delicacies we hadn't seen in ages—and were escorted to our "cabins." Three hundred women were assigned to a compart-ment on one deck, and over three hundred men to another deck.

At about midnight, we sailed for America. About an hour later, all of us were sorry to have eaten that gourmet food: we were terribly seasick. We begged for salty or sour food, but all we were served for the next two weeks were sweet, bland meals—food we couldn't even bare to look at. Julie came to visit me and brought salty crackers, which tasted heavenly, but he looked gaunt and ghostly himself.

When a storm hit the ship, it did extensive damage and left the passengers looking like ghosts, and those who could walk did so but swayed like drunks. Even some of the sailors suffered seasickness, holding on to ropes and walking dazedly.

We arrived in New York on Friday evening, January 24, 1947, and two weeks later Julie and I were married by an ultra-Orthodox rabbi. Julie went to work, learning a new trade and learning about American equipment, all the while declaring, "I am not afraid. I will work. I will build a new life, a new home." And that he did.

I went to work in the garment district. I had never held a needle in my hand, so the foreman taught me how to stitch a stiff canvas lining onto the lapels of men's suits. I started out hand-sewing one jacket a day and, when I had progressed to completing five a day, I asked for piecework, thinking this would mean more money. The foreman had a good laugh; the row of ancient Italian women produced about eighty jackets *an hour*. Their hands flew as they worked. It was like watching the spokes on a turning wheel—no spoke was visible individually.

After three months I got a job in the office of Polish Research and Information Services, and that lasted until a job that offered more benefits came my way: a full-time job at home. My children were born—and with them, joy flooded our lives. My earliest spoken words to them were, "You will claim my love. I have so much of it in my heart, now my outstretched arms can embrace not empty air but living love. With Daddy's protective love and in the warmth of a family, I feel whole now."

Julie believed in fairness, a quality to be admired and respected in a man. If the truth hurt, it had to be faced; right had to prevail and wrong had to be righted. Julie was not religious, but he held strongly to tradition. He was the one who prepared the Sabbath candles for Friday nights, admonishing me, "Don't be late for the lighting." Every Kaddish prayer for the dead was scrupulously and observed even in the last years of his illness I heard his strong commanding voice: "I want Shabbos observed." I could feel a chilling urgency in his voice.

Ever since he saw those ten rabbis on the lampposts in Lwów, hanged by the Nazis, there was a war going on inside Julie. First, "Why, God?" then, "No. Man, not God, did this to man." Julie came from an Orthodox home where he was reared in an atmosphere of love and respect for religion. While rebelling against it, however, it remained with him. God help anyone who made a disparaging remark about Chasidim in Julie's presence; they would pay a price for that. "This is their belief," he would say. "They have the right to their way of life. It should be respected as all people should be treated with the same civility." That was Julie's creed.

Julie had men of various backgrounds working for him in his metal-work business: Jews, Blacks, Spanish, Chinese—even a Pole who was a newcomer to this country. They were average, honest mechanics but communication, necessary among them in their work, was sometimes difficult. For example, the Pole spoke no English, and small verbal skirmishes inevitably broke out. The Black and Spanish men, in particular, often teased Jan, the Pole, and made uncivil remarks to and about him. Julie controlled the situation with strong words: "I will not have this kind of persecution in my shop. You all must speak English and teach it to Jan. From now on, you must say, 'Hand me the hammer' in English. Point to it and name it." A truce followed and peaceful work continued. Jan was obstinate, however, about his Polish. In the end, everyone in the shop learned to speak fairly fluent Polish.

Finally I decided to write my memoirs. "During those years of moral darkness . . ." I began, and paused for a moment to further articulate my thoughts. I did not notice that I had stopped writing and was staring into the past. I had opened a deep, dark cave that I truly feared to enter, for there, in that cave, was all the heartbreak, and it was passing before my eyes.

But I persevered and, as I went into that cave, all my sorrow and all my anger at Hitler and his henchmen spilled onto paper. I wrote with fire in my heart and, after several chapters had been completed and my fury spent, I was exhausted. I asked Julie to read the first draft of those early chapters. Bringing the hurt out of my heart calmed and helped me see that, actually, the first draft of those early chapters were not yet "fit to print."

Julie shook his head. "No, you cannot blame all of them. There were good people, too, people who helped us or at least tried to help." After we talked at length, he repeated his comment and gave the example of his Ukrainian friend who had provided him with Christian papers. He also cited Gentiles who had performed small but helpful deeds for him while he was on the run from Lwów. As he read each chapter, he offered gentle and constructive criticism.

I agreed with Julie: not all the people were bad. While the majority watched the horrors with glee and even participated in them, and while others looked on passively, indifferent to our appeals for help, there were those compassionate, caring, good people who honestly tried to respond to our needs. There were the Supczaks, the Wasiks, Pani Blawadowa, and the Polish boys who rescued me from the killing field. Even Mr. Orsiawski was basically a good person at heart. Other cases of people with sympathetic feelings for the downtrodden include a young Ukrainian man who searched for Jews in a cornfield, offered them a basket of food, and then took them into hiding. There was the German who let Bronia Hofman and her mother live by firing into the air and urging them to run. There were those who did nothing more than throw a piece of bread to a stranger, a Jew, and then in the same breath told him to disappear. And there was yet another German, one of the few whose hearts were not made of stone— the officer who tried to help my father's sister, Ronia, for example. When she and her three daughters (two adults and a twelve-year-old) had been caught in an akcja and herded into the marketplace in Przemysl, they had to wait under German and Ukrainian guard until the akcja was over so there would be enough victims to fill the cattle wagons to capacity and send them to their deaths. According to Cyla Reisher, a surviving relative of Ronia's husband who witnessed this incident, a German SS man brushed by Ronia and her daughters at one point during this long and torturous wait. After a short conversation with the women, the German motioned to the youngest girl and plainly told her to disappear. When she was obviously reluctant to leave, the man looked at the mother with an expression that clearly said, "Tell her to go," and prodded, almost pushed, the child to leave. Little Tunusia would not leave her mother and sisters, however, and cried and clung to her mother. The young child went to her death, embraced by her loving family, despite the German's offer of escape.

Yes, these were good people—exceptions in a sea of hostility. It is sad that there were so few. With respect and appreciation, we acknowledge all those rescuers, those small cells of righteous people. And I repeat my own and our collective Jewish gratitude to those same individuals, families, groups, and friends in need who, thinking with their hearts and healthy minds, believed that to be human is to have a conscience.

Many survivors from Buczacz, as well as from other territories held by the Nazis, are no longer with us and, as time passes, more will leave us. Over the years, some of us have spoken of the War years; some of us have remained silent. Eventually however, as we age, our pain and grief pour out. It might happen privately or at gatherings, such as bar mitzvahs or weddings. Many of us have witnessed such outpourings. At a wedding, for example, a voice at the end of a table half pleaded, half commanded, "Tonight, we do not talk of the Hitler years. Tonight we celebrate life," and heads nodded in agreement all around the room. Later, as the evening wore on and we progressed from small talk to discussions about whom to vote for—the Democrats or Nixon—and about the beautiful bride who was going to travel to Israel, and about the peace accord between Egypt and Israel, a dancing couple passed the table and stopped in their tracks. The man said, "Meyer, Meyer, how are you? You came from Canada? We were in prison together. *Men hot uns geshlugen un geharget.* They beat us and murdered us." He talked with growing animation to Meyer, his wife, and all the guests at the table, gesticulating to everyone. "After the typhus, after the liquidation, I went to Stach and Marynka. Peasants who patronized my father's store, they saved me in their potato cellar. *Gute Goyim.* Do you remember?" And suddenly the floodgates of memories of the Hitler years opened.

Now that the years are passing, all I ask of you, my dear children, is to remember that tragic chapter of our history. Guide yourselves by your forebears' fundamental principle: human integrity. Remember your lost family, for this book is the only monument for their graves. Remember, too, all those who lived and died during the Holocaust in Europe, for this book is their monument as well.

GLOSSARY

Words whose meaning is clear from the text are generally excluded.

Word or Name	Pronounced	Definition
akcja	act-tse-ah	"action," organized raid; pogrom
Arbeit	arbyt	work
Arbeitsamt	arbytsamt	employment office
Avinu Malkeinu	Avinoo Malkainoo	our father, our king (refers to God)
Banderowcy	Banderov'tseh	loyal followers of Bandera, a leader fighting for the independence of Ukraine
bar mitzvah	(as written)	a rite at which a thirteen-year-old boy becomes an adult member of the community
borscht	borsht	beet soup
briczka	britchka	small one-horse carriage
cheder	khay'der	room or place for religious study
Endecks	(as written)	a radical, militant, fiercely anti-Semitic party
Gemura	Gemoora	a compilation of discussions and comments in the Mishna; Gemura and Mishna make up the Talmud
gimnazjum/ gimnazja	jim-nazeeum/ jim-nazeeah	secondary school, high school
guter mensch	gooter mentsh	a good person
Jósefówka	yo'zeh'fuvkah	A Polish village

judenfrei	yooden-frai	literally "Free of Jews" in German
Judenrat	yooden-raht	Jewish Council
Kaddish	kahdish	prayer for the dead
kareta	(as written)	carriage
Kehilla	ke-heelah	literally, "community"
Kilim	keelim	rug hung on a wall
Kinder	kinder	"children" in Yiddish and German
Kol Nidre	kol needrei	opening words of the evening service commencing the Day of Atonement
Landsmanschaft	lahnds-mahn-shaft	association of compatriots
Mamusiu	mah'moo'sheoo	familiar term for "Mother"
mensch	mentch	literally, person; figuratively, humane person encompassing all best attributes
mincha-ma'arev	minha-maarev	afternoon prayers
mitzvah	(as written)	literally, "commandment"; figuratively, good deed or blessing
oblawa	ohb'la'vah	roundup of Jews
Pesach	Pesakh	Passover holiday
Purim	Poorim	holiday commemorating the deliverance of Jews from extermination in Persia
pogrom	poh'grom	raid on a Jewish Community
rejestracja	reh-yeh-strats-eeyah	"Registration"
shadchen	shatkhen	matchmaker
Shmoneh esreh	Shmonei esrei	eighteen benedictions, prayers spoken standing in silence
Shochet/Shekita	sho-khet/she-khita	ritual slaughterer for Kosher meat/ritual slaughtering
shtetl	shtet-ul	Eastern European Jewish village

soyuz	(as written)	cooperative grocery
Talmud	talmood	unique literary work by scholars in academies of Palestine and Babylonia, the result of study over eight centuries
Talmud–Torah	talmood-toe-rah	place for learning Torah
Tarbut	tar-boot	literally, "culture"
Tatko	Tat-ko	familiar term for "Father"
thephillin	tefeelin	phylactery; a strap of special leather wound around the left forearm, worn by Jewish men for weekday morning services
Torah	toe-rah	the "law," first five books of the Bible
Yad VaShem	yaad va shaym	Israeli Museum of the Holocaust
Yizkor	yiskor	memorial service prayer for repose of the dead
Yom Kippur	yom kipoor	Day of Atonement